Alfred Taylor, John Barry Simmons

The Tabernacle Chorus

Alfred Taylor, John Barry Simmons

The Tabernacle Chorus

ISBN/EAN: 9783337345723

Printed in Europe, USA, Canada, Australia, Japan

Cover: Foto ©Thomas Meinert / pixelio.de

More available books at **www.hansebooks.com**

THE
TABERNACLE CHORUS.

[TRINITY EDITION.]

COMPILED BY

REV. ALFRED TAYLOR
AND
J. B. SIMMONS, D.D.

"Make a joyful noise unto the Lord, all the earth: make a loud noise, and rejoice, and sing praise. Psalm 98. 4."

NEW YORK:
PUBLISHED BY BIGLOW & MAIN,
76 EAST NINTH STREET.
1877.

Copyright, 1877, by BIGLOW & MAIN.

HYMNS AND TUNES

SPECIALLY ADAPTED TO EACH OTHER.

Hymn	Book	Page	Hymn	Book	Page
21	Songs of Devotion...	110	109	Songs of Devotion...	74
25	Songs of Salvation...	140	113	Songs of Devotion...	69
28	Songs of Devotion...	22	116	Songs of Salvation...	88
32	Plymouth Collection	433	118	Songs of Devotion...	208
37	Songs of Devotion...	33	124	Hallowed Songs.....	2
41	Songs of Devotion...	102	127	Songs of Devotion...	73
72	The Charm..........	21	134	Songs of Devotion...	125
75	Songs of Devotion...	213	135	Songs of Salvation..	182
80	Songs of Salvation..	115	140	Songs of Devotion...	103
83	Songs of Devotion...	152	161	Hallowed Songs.....	77
85	Songs of Devotion...	153	177	Songs of Devotion...	24
92	Fresh Laurels.......	20	184	Songs of Devotion...	248
103	Songs of Salvation...	70	185	Songs of Salvation...	22
108	Songs of Salvation...	86			

The books above mentioned may be purchased of BIGLOW & MAIN, 76 East Ninth-street, New York.

INTRODUCTION.

OUR idea is to put in small space, with comfortable type, the old and new hymns which are so "catching" that a congregation cannot help but sing. Not more than one out of four church-goers sings, and he who does sing is apt to do it with his mouth half shut, as though to keep his soul from escaping with the utterance.

We do not print the music with the words, because the vast majority of people in church never look at the music even when it is printed. Besides that, nearly all the tunes we sing are familiar, and we need no guideboard on a road we have all our lives been travelling. If there be any one who does not know "Toplady" and "Antioch," we defy all the music books of the world to teach him. When we want to employ "new tunes" we will learn them in the congregational singing-school, an indispensable institution. The "notes" are indispensable for schools where the art is to be learned; but if in church one cannot follow a tune except by poising himself on minims or semi-quavers, there will not be much devotion in what he sings. It makes us nervous to have a man sitting next to us in church who sings by note when he does not know how. Instead of mounting heavenward on the five-runged ladder of the musical staff, he is all the time afraid of falling off. We do not come to church to study music, but to worship God.

INTRODUCTION.

We also want a cheap book, so that if there be ten members of a family, there can be ten copies in a pew, that number costing no more than one copy of the ordinarily expensive Church Hymn Book.

We hear on all sides a demand for such a publication, and to supply that, while at the same time we gratify our own congregation, we send this unpretending volume forth with the prayer, "Let every thing that hath breath praise the Lord!"

T. DE WITT TALMAGE.

BROOKLYN, *Feb.* 22, 1874.

THESE two hundred choice hymns, which are enough to last any congregation for a long time, are arranged in alphabetical order. This affords much greater convenience for finding them, than if arranged according to their subjects.

An ample *Index of Subjects* is at the end of the book, as well as an *Index of First Lines*.

On page 2 will be found an *Index of Special Tunes* adapted to the hymns of irregular metre. This furnishes every needed facility for the use of all those hymns. The other hymns can be sung to well-known tunes, concerning which no particular direction is needed.

Compilers of other hymn books are reminded that many of the hymns in this book are copyright property, which must not be taken without consent of the publishers.

A. T.

Tabernacle Chorus.

1   S. M.

Watch.—MATT. 25. 13.

A CHARGE to keep I have,
   A God to glorify;
A never-dying soul to save,
   And fit it for the sky.

2 To serve the present age,
   My calling to fulfil,
O, may it all my powers engage
   To do my Master's will.

3 Arm me with jealous care,
   As in thy sight to live;
And O, thy servant, Lord, prepare
   A strict account to give.

4 Help me to watch and pray,
   And on thyself rely,
Assured, if I my trust betray,
   I shall forever die.

2   C. M.

Christ died for our sins.—1 COR. 15. 3.

ALAS! and did my Saviour bleed!
   And did my Sov'reign die!
Would he devote that sacred head
   For such a worm as I?

Tabernacle Chorus.

2 Was it for crimes that I have done,
 He groaned upon the tree?
Amazing pity! grace unknown!
 And love beyond degree!

3 Well might the sun in darkness hide
 And shut his glories in;
When Christ, the mighty Maker, died
 For man the creature's sin.

4 Thus might I hide my blushing face,
 While his dear cross appears:
Dissolve my heart in thankfulness,
 And melt mine eyes to tears.

5 But drops of grief can ne'er repay
 The debt of love I owe;
Here, Lord, I give myself away,
 'Tis all that I can do.

3   C. M.

God is faithful, who will not suffer you to be tempted above that ye are able.—1 Cor. 10. 13.

ALAS! what hourly dangers rise,
 What snares beset my way;
To heaven, O let me lift mine eyes,
 And hourly watch and pray.

2 Whene'er temptations fright my heart,
 Or lure my feet aside,
My God, thy powerful aid impart,
 My Guardian and my Guide.

3 O keep me in thy heavenly way,
 And bid the tempter flee;
And let me never, never stray,
 From happiness and thee.

Tabernacle Chorus.

4   C. M.
King of kings, and Lord of lords.—Rev. 19. 16.

ALL hail the power of Jesus' name!
  Let angels prostrate fall;
Bring forth the royal diadem,
  And crown him Lord of all.

2 Ye chosen seed of Israel's race,
  Ye ransomed from the fall,
Hail him, who saves you by his grace,
  And crown him Lord of all.

3 Sinners, whose love can ne'er forget
  The wormwood and the gall,
Go, spread your trophies at his feet,
  And crown him Lord of all.

4 Let every kindred, every tribe,
  On this terrestrial ball,
To him all majesty ascribe,
  And crown him Lord of all.

5 O that with yonder sacred throng,
  We at his feet may fall;
We 'll join the everlasting song,
  And crown him Lord of all.

5   C. M.
Being justified freely by his grace.—Romans 3. 24.

AMAZING grace! how sweet the sound
  That saved a wretch like me!
I once was lost, but now am found;
  Was blind, but now I see.

2 'Twas grace that taught my heart to fear,
  And grace my fears relieved:
How precious did that grace appear,
  The hour I first believed!

Tabernacle Chorus.

3 Through many dangers, toils, and snares
   I have already come:
'Tis grace that brought me safe thus far,
   And grace will lead me home.

4 And when this flesh and heart shall fail,
   And mortal life shall cease,
I shall possess, within the vail,
   A life of joy and peace.

6   C. M.

Fight the good fight of faith.—1 Tim. 6. 12.

AM I a soldier of the cross,
   A foll'wer of the Lamb?
And shall I fear to own his cause,
   Or blush to speak his name?

2 Must I be carried to the skies,
   On flowery beds of ease?
While others fought to win the prize,
   And sailed through bloody seas?

3 Are there no foes for me to face?
   Must I not stem the flood?
Is this vile world a friend to grace,
   To help me on to God?

4 Sure, I must fight, if I would reign:
   Increase my courage, Lord!
I'll bear the toil, endure the pain,
   Supported by the word.

5 Thy saints, in all this glorious war,
   Shall conquer, though they die;
They see the triumph from afar,
   By faith they bring it nigh.

Tabernacle Chorus.

6 When that illustrious day shall rise,
    And all thine armies shine
In robes of victory through the skies,
    The glory shall be thine.

7   S. M.

We shall all stand before the judgment seat of Christ
    Romans 14. 10.

AND will the Judge descend?
    And must the dead arise?
And not a single soul escape
    His all-discerning eyes?

2 How will my heart endure
    The terrors of that day,
When earth and heaven before his face
    Astonished shrink away?

3 But ere the trumpet shakes
    The mansions of the dead,
Hark! from the Gospel's cheering sound,
    What joyful tidings spread.

4 Ye sinners, seek his grace,
    Whose wrath ye cannot bear;
Fly to the shelter of his cross,
    And find salvation there.

8   C. M.

O God, hear the prayer of thy servant.—Dan. 9. 17.

APPROACH, my soul, the mercy-seat,
    Where Jesus answers prayer;
There humbly fall before his feet,
    For none can perish there.

Tabernacle Chorus.

2 Thy promise is my only plea;
  With this I venture nigh;
Thou callest burdened souls to thee,
  And such, O Lord, am I.

3 Bow'd down beneath a load of sin,
  By Satan sorely press'd,
By war without, and fear within,
  I come to thee for rest.

4 Be thou my shield and hiding-place;
  That, shelter'd near thy side,
I may my fierce accuser face,
  And tell him, Thou hast died.

5 O, wondrous love! to bleed and die,
  To bear the cross and shame,
That guilty sinners, such as I,
  Might plead thy gracious Name!

9   H. M.

Seeing he ever liveth to make intercession for them.
HEB. 7. 25.

ARISE, my soul, arise;
  Shake off thy guilty fears;
The bleeding sacrifice
  In my behalf appears;
Before the throne my surety stands:
My name is written on his hands.

2 He ever lives above,
    For me to intercede,
  His all-redeeming love,
    His precious blood to plead;
His blood atoned for all our race,
And sprinkles now the throne of grace.

Tabernacle Chorus.

3 My God is reconciled;
　His pardoning voice I hear;
He owns me for his child—
　I can no longer fear;
His Spirit answers to the blood,
And tells me I am born of God

10　　　　　　　　　　L. M.
Awake, awake; put on strength, O arm of the Lord.—
Isaiah 51. 9.

ARM of the Lord, awake, awake,
　Put on thy strength, the nations shake.
And let the world, adoring, see
Triumphs of mercy wrought by thee.

2 Say to the heathen, from thy throne,
"I am Jehovah—God alone:"
Thy voice their idols shall confound,
And cast their altars to the ground.

3 No more let human blood be spilt,
Vain sacrifice for human guilt;
But to each conscience be applied
The blood that flowed from Jesus' side.

4 Almighty God, thy grace proclaim,
In every land declare thy name,
Let adverse powers before thee fall,
And crown the Saviour—LORD OF ALL.

11　　　　　　　　　　S. M.
They sing the song of Moses the servant of God, and
　the song of the Lamb.—Rev. 15. 3.

AWAKE, and sing the song
　Of Moses and the Lamb;
Wake every heart and every tongue!
　To praise the Saviour's name.

Tabernacle Chorus.

2 Sing of his dying love:
   Sing of his rising power;
Sing—how he intercedes above
   For those whose sins he bore.

3 Ye pilgrims! on the road
   To Zion's city, sing!
Rejoice ye in the Lamb of God,—
   In Christ, the eternal King.

4 Soon shall we hear him say,—
   "Ye blessed children! come;"
Soon will he call us hence away,
   And take his wanderers home.

5 There shall each raptured tongue
   His endless praise proclaim;
And sweeter voices tune the song
   Of Moses and the Lamb.

12   L. M.

I will sing aloud of thy mercy in the morning.
    Psa. 59. 16.

AWAKE, my soul, and with the sun
   Thy daily course of duty run;
Shake off dull sloth, and early rise
To pay thy morning sacrifice.

2 Wake, and lift up thyself, my heart,
And with the angels bear thy part;
Who all night long unwearied sing,
"Glory to thee, eternal King."

3 Glory to thee, who safe hast kept
And hast refreshed me while I slept;
Grant, Lord, when I from death shall wake,
I may of endless life partake.

Tabernacle Chorus.

4 Lord, I my vows to thee renew;
Scatter my sins as morning dew;
Guard my first spring of thought and will,
And with thyself my spirit fill.

5 Direct, control, suggest this day,
All I design, or do, or say,
That all my powers, with all their might,
In thy sole glory may unite.

13   L. M.

*How excellent is thy loving-kindness!—*Psa. 86. 7.

AWAKE, my soul, in joyful lays,
  And sing thy great Redeemer's praise.
He justly claims a song from thee,—
His loving-kindness, O how free!

2 He saw me ruined in the fall,
Yet loved me, notwithstanding all.
He saved me from my lost estate,—
His loving-kindness, O how great!

3 When trouble, like a gloomy cloud,
Has gathered thick, and thundered loud,
He near my soul has always stood,—
His loving-kindness, O how good!

4 Soon shall I pass the gloomy vale,
Soon all my mortal powers must fail;
O! may my last expiring breath
His loving-kindness sing in death.

5 Then let me mount and soar away
To the bright world of endless day;
And sing with rapture and surprise,
His loving-kindness in the skies.

Tabernacle Chorus.

14   C. M.

*I press toward the mark for the prize of the high calling of God in Christ Jesus.—*Phil. 3. 14.

AWAKE, my soul, stretch every nerve,
  And press with vigour on:
A heavenly race demands thy zeal,
  And an immortal crown.

2 A cloud of witnesses around
  Hold thee in full survey;
Forget the steps already trod,
  And onward urge thy way.

3 'Tis God's all animating voice
  That calls thee from on high;
'Tis his own hand presents the prize
  To thine uplifted eye.

4 Then wake, my soul, stretch every nerve,
  And press with vigour on;
A heavenly race demands thy zeal,
  And an immortal crown.

15   L. M.

Make a joyful noise unto the Lord, all ye lands.
Psa. 100. 1.

BEFORE Jehovah's awful throne
  Ye nations bow with sacred joy;
Know that the Lord is God alone,—
  He can create, and he destroy.

2 His sov'reign power, without our aid,
  Made us of clay, and form'd us men;
And when, like wand'ring sheep, we stray'd
  He brought us to His fold again.

Tabernacle Chorus.

3 We are thy people, we thy care;
  Our souls and all our mortal frame:
What lasting honours shall we rear,
  Almighty Maker, to thy name!

4 We'll crowd thy gates with thankful songs;
  High as the heavens our voices raise:
And earth, with her ten thousand tongues,
  Shall fill thy courts with sounding praise.

5 Wide as the world is thy command,
  Vast as eternity thy love;
Firm as a rock thy truth must stand,
  When rolling years shall cease to move.

16   L. M.
Behold, I stand at the door, and knock.—REV. 3. 20.

BEHOLD a stranger at the door;
  He gently knocks, has knocked before;
Hath waited long,—is waiting still;
You treat no other friend so ill.

2 O, lovely attitude! He stands
With melting heart and outstretched hands!
O, matchless kindness! and he shows
This matchless kindness to his foes!

3 Admit him, ere his anger burn,
His feet departed ne'er return;
Admit him, or the hour's at hand,
You'll at his door rejected stand.

17   S. M.
Behold the Lamb of God!—JOHN 1. 29.

BEHOLD the Lamb of God,
  Who takes my sin away,
And, cleansing me in precious blood,
  Leaves naught for me to pay.

Tabernacle Chorus.

2 The sin-atoning Lamb,
  The Sacrifice for me;
Pardoned and justified I am,
  From condemnation free.

3 My Saviour and my God
  Was crucified for me;
For me he shed his precious blood
  Upon the cursed tree.

4 He died my soul to save—
  How rich, how free his love!
Through him I triumph o'er the grave,
  And reign with him above.

18   11, 8.
Know ye that the Lord he is God.—Psa. 100. 3.

BE joyful in God, all ye lands of the earth;
  Oh, serve him with gladness and fear;
Exult in his presence with music and mirth;
  With love and devotion draw near.

2 For Jehovah is God, and Jehovah alone,
    Creator and Ruler o'er all;
And we are his people, his sceptre we own;
    His sheep, and we follow his call.

3 Oh, enter his gates with thanksgiving and
      song;
    Your vows in his temple proclaim;
His praise with melodious accordance prolong,
    And bless his adorable name.

4 For good is the Lord, inexpressibly good,
    And we are the work of his hand;
His mercy and truth from eternity stood,
    And shall to eternity stand.

Tabernacle Chorus.

19 S. M.
We are one body in Christ.—Rom. 12. 5.

BLEST be the tie that binds
  Our hearts in Christian love,—
The fellowship of kindred minds
  Is like to that above.

2 Before our Father's throne
  We pour our ardent prayers;
Our fears, our hopes, our aims are one,
  Our comforts, and our cares.

3 We share our mutual woes,
  Our mutual burdens bear,
And often for each other flows
  The sympathizing tear.

4 The glorious hope revives
  Our courage by the way,
While each in expectation lives,
  And longs to see the day.

5 From sorrow, toil, and pain,
  And sin, we shall be free;
And perfect love and friendship reign
  Through all eternity.

20 H. M.
In the day of atonement shall ye make the trumpet sound.—Lev. 25. 9.

BLOW ye the trumpet, blow
  The gladly solemn sound;
Let all the nations know,
  To earth's remotest bound,
The year of Jubilee is come,
Return, ye ransomed sinners, home.

Tabernacle Chorus.

2 Exalt the Lamb of God,
    The sin-atoning Lamb;
Redemption by his blood
    Through all the lands proclaim;
The year of Jubilee is come;
Return, ye ransomed sinners, home.

3 Ye who have sold for naught
    The heritage above,
Shall have it back unbought,
    The gift of Jesus' love;
The year of Jubilee is come;
Return, ye ransomed sinners, home.

4 The gospel trumpet hear,
    The news of pard'ning grace;
Ye happy souls, draw near,
    Behold your Saviour's face:
The year of Jubilee is come;
Return, ye ransomed sinners, home.

21   11, 10.

We have seen his star in the east, and are come to worship him.—MATT. 2. 2.

BRIGHTEST and best of the sons of the morning,
    Dawn on our darkness and lend us thine aid!
Star of the East, the horizon adorning,
    Guide where our infant Redeemer is laid.

2 Cold on his cradle the dewdrops are shining,
    Low lies his head with the beasts of the stall;
Angels adore him in slumber reclining,
    Maker, and Monarch, and Saviour of all.

Tabernacle Chorus.

3 Say, shall we yield him, in costly devotion,
   Odours of Edom and off'rings divine?
Gems of the mountain, and pearls of the ocean,
   Myrrh from the forest, or gold from the mine?

4 Vainly we offer each ample oblation;
   Vainly with gifts would his favour secure;
Richer by far is the heart's adoration;
   Dearer to God are the prayers of the poor.

CHORUS:

Hallelujah to the Lamb, who has purchased
   our pardon;
We'll praise him again when we pass over
   Jordan.

22   L. M.

Enter ye in at the strait gate.—MATT. 7. 13.

BROAD is the road that leads to death,
   And thousands walk together there;
But wisdom shows a narrow path,
   With here and there a traveller.

2 "Deny thyself and take thy cross,"
   Is the Redeemer's great command:
Nature must count her gold but dross,
   If she would gain this heavenly land.

3 The fearful soul that tires and faints,
   And walks the ways of God no more,
Is but esteemed almost a saint,
   And makes his own destruction sure.

4 Lord! let not all my hopes be vain:
   Create my heart entirely new:
Which hypocrites could ne'er attain,
   Which false apostates never knew.

Tabernacle Chorus

23 C. M.

Peace with God through our Lord Jesus Christ.
Rom. 5. 1.

CALM me, my God, and keep me calm;
  Let thine outstretchéd wing
Be like the shade of Elim's palm,
  Beside her desert spring.

2 Yes, keep me calm, though loud and rude
  The sounds my ear that greet,—
Calm in the closet's solitude,
  Calm in the bustling street,—

3 Calm in the hour of buoyant health,
  Calm in the hour of pain,
Calm in my poverty or wealth,
  Calm in my loss or gain,—

4 Calm in the sufferance of wrong,
  Like Him who bore my shame,
Calm 'mid the threat'ning, taunting throng,
  Who hate thy holy name.

5 Calm me, my God, and keep me calm,
  Soft resting on thy breast;
Soothe me with holy hymn and psalm,
  And bid my spirit rest. -

24 7s.

Rejoice in the Lord always.—Phil. 4. 4.

CHILDREN of the heavenly King!
  As we journey, let us sing;
Sing our Saviour's worthy praise,
Glorious in his works and ways.

Tabernacle Chorus.

2 We are travelling home to God,
In the way the fathers trod;
They are happy now, and we
Soon their happiness shall see.

3 Shout, ye little flock, and blest;
You on Jesus' throne shall rest,
There, your seat is now prepared,
There, your kingdom and reward.

4 Fear not, brethren, joyful stand
On the borders of our land;
Jesus Christ, our Father's Son,
Bids us undismay'd go on.

5 Lord! obediently we'll go,
Gladly leaving all below;
Only thou our leader be,
And we still will follow thee.

25   7s.

Now is Christ risen from the dead.—1 Cor. 15. 20.

CHRIST is risen from the dead,
  Christ, our ever-living Head;
Now he lives who once was slain,
Lives, for evermore to reign.
Risen Sun of Righteousness,
Risen to save, to cheer, to bless;
Blessed Saviour, living Lord,
Ever be thy name adored.

      CHORUS:
Mighty Victor, strong to save,
Thou hast conquered o'er the grave.
Death hath lost its power and sting;
Praise to our victorious King.

Tabernacle Chorus.

2 Christ hath triumphed o'er the grave:
Christ hath shown his power to save.
Cruel death, and bitter strife—
Christ hath purchased endless life.
Now our faith is not in vain;
Jesus Christ hath risen again:
Vict'ry through our conquering Lord,
To his Father's throne restored.

3 Bright our hope beyond the tomb,
Gone the darkness, gone the gloom;
Gone the dreadful fear of death;
We may sing with latest breath.
Sown in weakness, raised in power,
For the resurrection hour;
Glory, glory, let us sing,
Glory to our risen King.

26 7s.

Seek those things which are above, where Christ sitteth on the right hand of God.—Col. iii. 1.

CHRIST the Lord is risen to-day,
Sons of men and angels say:
Raise your joys and triumphs high,
Sing, ye heavens, and earth reply.

2 Love's redeeming work is done,
Fought the fight, the vict'ry won:
Jesus' agony is o'er,
Darkness veils the earth no more.

3 Vain the stone, the watch, the seal,
Christ has burst the gates of hell;
Death in vain forbids him rise,
Christ hath opened Paradise.

Tabernacle Chorus.

4 Soar we now where Christ hath led,
Following our exalted Head;
Made like him, like him we rise;
Ours the cross, the grave, the skies.

27   L. M.

Be perfectly joined together in the same mind.
1 Cor. 1. 10.

COME, Christian brethren, ere we part,
   Join every voice and every heart;
One solemn hymn to God we raise,
One final song of grateful praise.

2 Christians, we here may meet no more,
But there is yet a happier shore;
And there, released from toil and pain,
Dear brethren, we shall meet again.

28

Your sins are forgiven you for his name's sake.
1 John 2. 12.

COME, come to Jesus!
   He waits to welcome thee,
O wand'rer, eagerly;
   Come, come to Jesus!

2 Come, come to Jesus!
   He waits to ransom thee,
O slave! eternally;
   Come, come to Jesus!

3 Come, come to Jesus!
   He waits to lighten thee,
O burdened! graciously;
   Come, come to Jesus!

Tabernacle Chorus.

4 Come, come to Jesus!
   He waits to give to thee,
O blind! a vision free;
   Ccme, come to Jesus!

29   H. M.

Blessed be his glorious name forever.—PSALM 72. 19.

COME, every pious heart
   That loves the Saviour's name,
Your noblest powers exert
   To celebrate his fame:
Tell all above and all below,
The debt of love to him you owe.

   2 He left his starry crown,
      And laid his robes aside;
On wings of love came down,
      And wept, and bled, and died.
What he endured, O! who can tell?
To save our souls from death and hell.

   3 From the dark grave he rose,
      The mansion of the dead;
And thence his mighty foes
      In glorious triumph led:
Up through the sky the conq'ror rode,
And reigns on high, the Saviour God.

   4 Jesus, we ne'er can pay
      The debt we owe thy love;
Yet tell us how we may
      Our gratitude approve:
Our hearts—our all to thee we give:
The gift, though small, do thou receive.

Tabernacle Chorus.

30   S. M.

He will guide you into all truth.—John 16. 13.

COME, Holy Spirit, come,
  Let thy bright beams arise;
Dispel the darkness from our minds,
  And open thou our eyes.

2 Revive our drooping faith,
  Our doubts and fears remove,
And kindle in our breasts the flame
  Of never-dying love.

3 'Tis thine to cleanse the heart,
  To sanctify the soul,
To pour fresh life on every part,
  And new create the whole.

4 Dwell, therefore, in our hearts,
  Our minds from bondage free;
Then shall we know, and praise, and love,
  The Father, Son, and thee.

31   C. M.

Quicken me, O Lord, for thy name's sake.—Psa. 143. 11.

COME, Holy Spirit, heavenly Dove,
  With all thy quick'ning powers:
Kindle a flame of sacred love
  In these cold hearts of ours.

2 In vain we tune our formal songs,
  In vain we strive to rise;
Hosannas languish on our tongues,
  And our devotion dies.

Tabernacle Chorus.

3 Dear Lord, and shall we ever live
　At this poor dying rate;
Our love so faint, so cold to thee,
　And thine to us so great?

4 Come, Holy Spirit, heavenly Dove,
　With all thy quick'ning powers;
Come, shed abroad a Saviour's love,
　And that shall kindle ours.

32

Now is our salvation nearer than when we believed.
ROMANS 13. 11.

COME, let us anew
　Our journey pursue,
Roll round with the year,
And never stand still till the Master appear.
　His adorable will
　Let us gladly fulfil,
And our talents improve
By the patience of hope and the labour of love.

2 Our life is a dream;
　Our time, as a stream,
Glides swiftly away,
And the fugitive moment refuses to stay.
　The arrow is flown,
　The moment is gone,
The millennial year
Rushes on to our view, and eternity's here.

3 O that each, in the day
　Of His coming, may say,
"I have fought my way through,
I have finished the work thou did'st give me
　　to do!"

Tabernacle Chorus.

O that each from his Lord
May receive the glad word,
"Well and faithfully done;
Enter into my joy, and sit down on my throne!"

33   C. M.
Worthy is the Lamb that was slain.—Rev. 5. 12.

COME, let us join our cheerful songs
  With angels round the throne;
Ten thousand thousand are their tongues,
  But all their joys are one.

2 "Worthy the Lamb that died," they cry,
  "To be exalted thus:"
"Worthy the Lamb," our hearts reply,
  "For he was slain for us."

3 Jesus is worthy to receive
  Honour and power divine;
And blessings, more than we can give,
  Be, Lord, forever thine.

34   L. M
And they sung a new song.—Rev. 5. 9.

COME, let us sing the song of songs-
  The saints in heaven began the strain—
The homage which to Christ belongs:
  "Worthy the Lamb, for he was slain!"

2 Slain to redeem us by his blood,
  To cleanse from every sinful stain,
And make us kings and priests to God—
  "Worthy the Lamb, for he was slain!"

Tabernacle Chorus.

3 To him who suffer'd on the tree,
　Our souls, at his soul's price to gain,
Blessing, and praise, and glory be:
　"Worthy the Lamb, for he was slain!"

4 To him, enthron'd by filial right,
　All power in heaven and earth proclaim,
Honour, and majesty, and might:
　"Worthy the Lamb, for he was slain!"

5 Long as we live, and when we die,
　And while in heaven with him we reign,
This song our song of songs shall be:
　"Worthy the Lamb, for he was slain!"

35　　　　　　　　　　H. M.
That Christ may dwell in your hearts by faith.
Eph. 3. 17.

COME, my Redeemer, come,
　And deign to dwell with me;
Come, and thy right assume,
　And bid thy rivals flee:
Come, my Redeemer, quickly come,
And make my heart thy lasting home.

2 Rule thou in every thought
　And passion of my soul,
Till all my powers are brought
　Beneath thy full control:
Come, my Redeemer, quickly come,
And make my heart thy lasting home.

3 Then shall my days be thine,
　And all my heart be love;
And joy and peace be mine,
　Such as are known above:
Come, my Redeemer, quickly come,
And make my heart thy lasting home.

Tabernacle Chorus.

36 C. M.

Behold, what manner of love the Father hath bestowed
   upon us.—1 John 3. 1.

COME, shout aloud the Father's grace,
   And sing the Saviour's love;
Soon shall we join the glorious theme,
   In loftier strains above.

2 God, the eternal, mighty God,
   To dearer names descends;
Calls us his treasure and his joy,
   His children and his friends.

3 My Father, God! and may these lips
   Pronounce a name so dear!
Not thus could heaven's sweet harmony
   Delight my listening ear.

4 Thanks to my God for every gift
   His bounteous hands bestow;
And thanks eternal for that love
   Whence all those comforts flow.

37 S. M.

And God shall wipe away all tears from their eyes.
   Rev. 21. 4.

COME sing to me of heaven
   When I'm about to die;
Sing songs of holy ecstasy,
   To waft my soul on high.

   Chorus:

   There'll be no more sorrow there,
   There'll be no more sorrow there,
      In heaven above,
      Where all is love,
   There'll be no more sorrow there.

Tabernacle Chorus.

2 When cold and sluggish drops
   Roll off my marble brow,
Burst forth in strains of joyfulness,
   Let heaven begin below.

3 When the last moments come,
   O watch my dying face,
To catch the bright seraphic glow
   Which in each feature plays.

4 Then to my raptured ear
   Let one sweet song be given;
Let music charm me last on earth,
   And greet me first in heaven.

5 When round my senseless clay,
   Assemble those I love,
Then sing of heaven, delightful heaven!
   My glorious home above!

38   6, 4.

O magnify the Lord with me, and let us exalt his name together.—PSA. 34. 3.

COME, thou almighty King,
   Help us thy name to sing,
      Help us to praise:
Father! all-glorious,
O'er all victorious,
Come, and reign over us,
      Ancient of Days!

2 Come, thou incarnate Word!
Gird on thy mighty sword;
      Our prayer attend;
Come, and thy people bless,
And give thy word success:
Spirit of holiness!
      On us descend.

Tabernacle Chorus.

3 Come, holy Comforter!
Thy sacred witness bear
   In this glad hour:
Thou, who almighty art,
Now rule in every heart,
And ne'er from us depart,
   Spirit of power!

4 To the great One in Three,
The highest praises be,
   Hence, evermore!
His sov'reign majesty
May we in glory see,
And to eternity
   Love and adore.

39   8, 7.
Hitherto hath the Lord helped us.—1 SAM. 7. 12.

COME, thou Fount of every blessing,
   Tune my heart to sing thy grace;
Streams of mercy, never ceasing,
   Call for songs of loudest praise;
Teach me some melodious sonnet,
   Sung by flaming tongues above;
Praise the mount—I'm fixed upon it!—
   Mount of thy redeeming love.

2 Here I'll raise mine Ebenezer;
   Hither by thy help I'm come;
And I hope, by thy good pleasure,
   Safely to arrive at home.
Jesus sought me when a stranger,
   Wandering from the fold of God;
He, to rescue me from danger,
   Interposed his precious blood.

Tabernacle Chorus.

3 O, to grace how great a debtor
   Daily I'm constrained to be!
Let thy goodness, like a fetter,
   Bind my wandering heart to thee.
Prone to wander, Lord, I feel it;
   Prone to leave the God I love;
Here's my heart; O, take and seal it;
   Seal it for thy courts above.

40   S. M.

The Lord will give grace and glory.—Psa. 84. 11.

COME, we who love the Lord,
   And let our joys be known;
Join in a song with sweet accord,
   And thus surround the throne.

2 Let those refuse to sing
   Who never knew our God;
But children of the heavenly King
   Should speak their joys abroad.

3 The men of grace have found
   Glory begun below:
Celestial fruits on earthly ground,
   From faith and hope may grow.

4 The hill of Zion yields
   A thousand sacred sweets
Before we reach the heavenly fields,
   Or walk the golden streets.

5 Then let our songs abound,
   And every tear be dry;
We're marching thro' Immanuel's ground
   To fairer worlds on high.

Tabernacle Chorus.

41
Is any among you afflicted? let him pray.—JAMES 5. 13.

COME, ye disconsolate, where'er ye languish,
  Come, at the mercy-seat fervently kneel:
Here bring your wounded hearts, here tell your anguish;
  Earth has no sorrow that heaven cannot heal.

2 Joy of the desolate, light of the straying,
  Hope of the penitent, fadeless and pure,
Here speaks the Comforter, in mercy saying,
  Earth has no sorrow that heaven cannot cure.

3 Here see the Bread of Life; see waters flowing
  Forth from the throne of God, pure from above;
Come to the feast of love—come, ever knowing
  Earth has no sorrow but heaven can remove.

42   7s.
He is able also to save them to the uttermost.—HEB. 7. 25.

DEPTH of mercy, can there be
  Mercy still reserved for me?
Can my God his wrath forbear?
Me, the chief of sinners, spare?

2 I have long withstood his grace,
Long provoked him to his face;
Would not hearken to his calls,
Grieved him by a thousand falls.

3 There for me the Saviour stands,
Shows his wounds, and spreads his hands
God is love! I know, I feel,
Jesus weeps, and loves me still.

Tabernacle Chorus.

4 Now incline me to repent!
Let me now my fall lament!
Now my foul revolt deplore,
Weep, believe, and sin no more.

43   S. M.

He beheld the city, and wept over it.—LUKE 19. 41.

DID Christ o'er sinners weep,
  And shall our cheeks be dry?
Let floods of penitential grief
  Burst forth from every eye.

2 The Son of God in tears,
  Angels with wonder see!
Be thou astonished, O my soul,
  He shed those tears for thee.

3 He wept that we might weep;
  Each sin demands a tear;
In heaven alone no sin is found,
  And there's no weeping there.

44   11s.

Him hath God exalted with his right hand to be a Prince and a Saviour.—ACTS 5. 31.

EXALTED Redeemer, almighty to save,
  Eternally victor o'er death and the grave,
To thee my thanksgiving I gratefully bring,
My Saviour, my Prince, my Omnipotent King.

2 Exalted, a Prince and a Saviour to reign,
In glory and light, till thou comest again;
Thou risen, ascended, victorious Lord
To the throne of thy Father in triumph restored.

Tabernacle Chorus.

3 Exalted, for me in thy mercy to plead,
To thee I draw near in the hour of my need·
On thine intercession alone I depend,
O Great Mediator, my Saviour, my Friend.

4 Exalted to sit on thy dread judgment-seat,
When all the earth's nations shall bow at thy feet :
Redeemer and Prince, Mediator and Friend,
Thy mercy will keep me secure to the end.

45   S. M.

And so shall we ever be with the Lord.—1 Thess. 4. 17.

FOREVER with the Lord!
  Amen, so let it be;
Life from the dead is in that word,
  'Tis immortality.

2 Here in the body pent,
  Absent from him I roam,
Yet nightly pitch my moving tent
  A day's march nearer home.

3 My Father's house on high,
  Home of my soul, how near
At times to Faith's illumined eye
  Thy golden gates appear!

4 My thirsty spirit faints
  To reach the land I love,
The bright inheri'ance of saints,
  Jerusalem above.

Tabernacle Chorus.

46 L. M. 6 l.
Even thine altars, O Lord of hosts, my King, and my God.—Psa. 84. 3.

FORTH from the dark and stormy sky,
Lord, to thine altar's shade we fly;
Forth from the world its hope and fear,
Father, we seek thy shelter here;
Weary and weak, thy grace we pray;
Turn not, O Lord, thy guests away.

2 Long have we roamed in want and pain,
Long have we sought thy rest in vain;
Wildered in doubt, in darkness lost,
Long have our souls been tempest-tossed:
Low at thy feet our sins we lay;
Turn not, O Lord, thy guests away.

47 L. M.
Let the people praise thee, O God; let ALL the people praise thee.—Psa. 67. 3.

FROM all that dwell below the skies,
Let the Creator's praise arise;
Let the Redeemer's name be sung
Through every land, by every tongue.

2 Eternal are thy mercies, Lord,
And truth eternal is thy word:
Thy praise shall sound from shore to shore,
Till suns shall rise and set no more.

48 L. M.
Let us draw near with a true heart.—Heb. 10. 22.

FROM every stormy wind that blows,
From every swelling tide of woes,
There is a calm, a sure retreat;
'Tis found before the mercy-seat.

Tabernacle Chorus.

2 There is a place where Jesus sheds
The oil of gladness on our heads,
A place of all on earth most sweet,
It is the blood-bought mercy-seat.

3 There is a scene where spirits blend,
Where friend holds fellowship with friend;
Though sundered far, by faith they meet
Around one common mercy-seat.

4 There, there on eagle wings we soar,
And sin and sense molest no more;
And heaven comes down our souls to greet,
And glory crowns the mercy-seat.

49   7, 6.

Go ye into all the world, and preach the gospel to every creature.—MARK 16. 15.

FROM Greenland's icy mountains,
  From India's coral strand,
Where Afric's sunny fountains
  Roll down their golden sand;
From many an ancient river,
  From many a palmy plain,
They call us to deliver
  Their land from error's chain.

2 What though the spicy breezes
  Blow soft o'er Ceylon's isle,
Though every prospect pleases,
  And only man is vile?
In vain with lavish kindness
  The gifts of God are strewn;
The heathen, in his blindness,
  Bows down to wood and stone.

Tabernacle Chorus.

3 Shall we whose souls are lighted
   With wisdom from on high,
Shall we, to men benighted,
   The lamp of life deny?
Salvation! O Salvation!
   The joyful sound proclaim,
Till earth's remotest nation
   Has learned Messiah's Name.

4 Waft, waft, ye winds, his story,
   And you, ye waters, roll,
Till, like a sea of glory,
   It spreads from pole to pole;
Till, o'er our ransomed nature,
   The Lamb for sinners slain,
Redeemer, King, Creator,
   In bliss returns to reign.

50   7s.

*Even so must the Son of man be lifted up: that whosoever believeth in him should not perish, but have eternal life.—*JOHN 3. 14, 15.

FROM the cross uplifted high,
Where the Saviour deigns to die,
What melodious sounds we hear,
Bursting on the ravished ear:
Love's redeeming work is done,
Come and welcome, sinner, come.

2 Sprinkled now with blood the throne,
Why beneath thy burdens groan!
On my piercéd body laid,
Justice owns the ransom paid;
Bow the knee and kiss the Son;
Come and welcome, sinner, come.

Tabernacle Chorus.

3 Spread for thee the festal board,
See with richest dainties stored;
To thy Father's bosom pressed,
Yet again a child confessed,
Never from his house to roam;
Come and welcome, sinner, come.

4 Soon the days of life shall end;
Lo! I come, your Saviour, Friend,
Safe your spirits to convey
To the realms of endless day,
Up to my eternal home;
Come and welcome, sinner, come.

51   S. M.

Trust ye in the Lord forever.—Isa. 26. 4.

GIVE to the winds thy fears;
    Hope, and be undismayed;
God hears thy sighs and counts thy tears,
    God shall lift up thy head.

2 Through waves, and clouds, and storms,
    He gently clears the way;
Wait thou his time; so shall this night
    Soon end in joyous day.

3 Still heavy is thy heart?
    Still sink thy spirits down?
Cast off the weight, let fear depart,
    And every care be gone.

4 What though thou rulest not?
    Yet heaven, and earth, and hell
Proclaim God sitteth on the throne,
    And ruleth all things well.

Tabernacle Chorus.

5 Leave to his sovereign sway,
　To choose and to command;
So shalt thou, wondering, own his way,
　How wise, how good his hand!

52　　　　　　　　　　6, 4.

Worthy is the Lamb that was slain.—Rev. 5. 12.

GLORY to God on high!
　Let heaven and earth reply,
　　Praise ye his name!
His love and grace adore,
Who all our sorrows bore;
Sing loud for evermore,
　　Worthy the Lamb!

2 While they around the throne
Cheerfully join in one,
　　Praising his name,—
Ye who have felt his blood
Sealing your peace with God,
Sound his dear name abroad,
　　Worthy the Lamb!

3 Join, all ye ransomed race,
Our Lord and God to bless:
　　Praise ye his name!
In him we will rejoice,
And make a joyful noise,
Shouting with heart and voice,
　　Worthy the Lamb!

4 Soon must we change our place,
Yet we will never cease
　　Praising his name·

Tabernacle Chorus.

To him our songs we bring;
Hail him our glorious King;
And, through all ages sing,
    Worthy the Lamb!

53   C. M.

How unsearchable are his judgments, and his ways past finding out!—Rom. 11. 33.

GOD moves in a mysterious way
  His wonders to perform;
He plants his footsteps in the sea,
  And rides upon the storm.

2 Deep in unfathomable mines,
  With never failing skill,
He treasures up his bright designs,
  And works his gracious will.

3 Ye fearful saints, fresh courage take;
  The clouds ye so much dread
Are big with mercy, and shall break
  In blessings on your head.

4 Judge not the Lord by feeble sense,
  But trust him for his grace;
Behind a frowning Providence
  He hides a smiling face.

5 His purposes will ripen fast,
  Unfolding every hour;
The bud may have a bitter taste,
  But sweet will be the flower.

6 Blind unbelief is sure to err,
  And scan his work in vain:
God is his own interpreter,
  And he will make it plain.

Tabernacle Chorus.

54   7s.

They shall call his name Emmanuel—God with us.
      MATT. 1. 23.

GOD with us! O, glorious name!
  Let it shine in endless fame;
God and man in Christ unite;
O, mysterious depth and height!

2 God with us! the eternal Son
Took our soul, our flesh, and bone;
Now, ye saints, his grace admire,
Swell the song with holy fire.

3 God with us! but tainted not
With the first transgressor's blot;
Yet did he our sins sustain,
Bear the guilt, the curse, the pain.

4 God with us! O, wondrous grace!
Let us see him face to face;
That we may Emmanuel sing,
As we ought, our God and King!

55   L. M.

Whoso putteth his trust in the Lord shall be safe.
      PROV. 29. 25.

GLORY to thee, my God, this night,
  For all the blessings of the light:
Keep me, O keep me, King of kings,
Under thine own Almighty wings.

2 Forgive me, Lord, for thy dear Son,
The ills that I this day have done:
That with the world, myself, and thee,
I, ere I sleep, at peace may be.

Tabernacle Chorus.

3 Teach me to live that I may dread
The grave as little as my bed;
Teach me to die, that so I may
Triumphing rise at the last day.

4 O may my soul on thee repose,
And with sweet sleep mine eyelids close:
Sleep, that may me more vig'rous make
To serve my God when I awake.

5 O when shall I, in endless day,
Forever chase dark sleep away,
And hymns divine with angels sing,
Glory to thee, eternal King?

56   S. M.

By grace are ye saved through faith.
Eph. 2. 8.

GRACE! 'tis a charming sound,
  Harmonious to the ear:
Heaven with the echo shall resound,
  And all the earth shall hear.

2 Grace first contrived a way
  To save rebellious man,
And all the means that grace display,
  Which drew the wondrous plan.

3 Grace guides my wandering feet
  To tread the heavenly road;
And new supplies each hour I meet
  While pressing on to God.

4 Grace all the work shall crown
  Through everlasting days;
It lays in heaven the topmost stone,
  And well deserves the praise.

Tabernacle Chorus.

57　　　　　　　　　　　　　　　　7s.

The earnest of the Spirit in our hearts.—2 Cor. 1. 22.

GRACIOUS Spirit, Love divine!
　Let thy light within me shine;
All my guilty fears remove;
Fill me with thy heavenly love.

2 Speak thy pard'ning grace to me,
Set the burden'd sinner free;
Lead me to the Lamb of God,
Wash me in his precious blood.

3 Life and peace to me impart,
Seal salvation on my heart;
Breathe thyself into my breast,—
Earnest of immortal rest.

4 Let me never from thee stray;
Keep me in the narrow way;
Fill my soul with joy divine;
Keep me, Lord, forever thine.

58　　　　　　　　　　　　　　　8, 7, 4

Praise ye the Lord.—Psa. 150. 1.

GREAT Jehovah, we adore thee,
　God the Father, God the Son,
God the Spirit, joined in glory
　On the same eternal throne:
　　Endless praises
　To Jehovah, Three in One.

Tabernacle Chorus.

59   8, 7, 4.

Thou shalt guide me with thy counsel.
Psa. 73. 24.

GUIDE me, O thou great Jehovah!
  Pilgrim through this barren land;
I am weak, but thou art mighty;
  Hold me with they powerful hand:
    Bread of heaven!
Feed me now and evermore.

2 Open now the crystal fountain,
  Whence the healing waters flow;
Let the fiery, cloudy pillar,
  Lead me all my journey through:
    Strong Deliv'rer,
Be thou still my strength and shield.

3 When I tread the verge of Jordan,
  Bid my anxious fears subside;
Thou of death and hell the conq'ror,
  Land me safe on Canaan's side:
    Songs of praises
  I will ever give to thee.

60   8, 7.

Who shall separate us from the love of Christ?
Romans 8. 35.

HAIL! my ever blessed Jesus,
  Only thee I wish to sing;
To my soul thy name is precious;
  Thou, my Prophet, Priest, and King.

2 O what mercy flows from heaven!
  O what joy and happiness!
Love I much? I'm much forgiven;
  I'm a miracle of grace.

Tabernacle Chorus.

3 Once with Adam's race in ruin,
    Unconcerned in sin I lay;
Swift destruction still pursuing,
    Till my Saviour passed that way.

4 Witness, all ye hosts of heaven,
    My Redeemer's tenderness;
Love I much? I'm much forgiven;
    I'm a miracle of grace.

5 Shout, ye bright angelic choir!
    Praise the Lamb enthron'd above;
Whilst, astonished, I admire
    God's free grace and boundless love.

6 That bless'd moment I received him
    Filled my soul with joy and peace:
Love I much? I'm much forgiven;
    I'm a miracle of grace.

61   7s.

Lovest thou me?—JOHN 21. 16.

HARK, my soul, it is the Lord;
'Tis thy Saviour, hear his word;
Jesus speaks, and speaks to thee:
Say, poor sinner, lov'st thou me?

2 I delivered thee when bound,
And when wounded healed thy wound;
Sought thee wandering, set thee right,
Turned thy darkness into light.

3 Mine is an unchanging love,
Higher than the heights above;
Deeper than the depths beneath,
Free and faithful, strong as death.

Tabernacle Chorus.

4 Thou shalt see my glory soon,
When the work of grace is done;
Partner of my throne shalt be;
Say, poor sinner, lov'st thou me?

5 Lord, it is my chief complaint
That my love is weak and faint;
Yet I love thee and adore;
O for grace to love thee more!

62   8, 7.

And cried with a loud voice, saying, Salvation to our God which sitteth upon the throne, and unto the Lamb.—Rev. 7. 10.

HARK, ten thousand harps and voices
    Sound the note of praise above;
Jesus reigns, and heaven rejoices:
    Jesus reigns, the God of love.
See! he sits on yonder throne!
Jesus rules the world alone!

2 Jesus, hail! whose glory brightens
    All above and gives it worth;
Lord of love, thy smile enlightens,
    Cheers and charms thy saints on earth;
When we think of love like thine,
Lord, we own it love divine.

3 King of glory, reign forever,
    Thine an everlasting crown;
Nothing from thy love shall sever
    Those whom thou hast made thine own;
Happy objects of thy grace,
Chosen to behold thy face.

Tabernacle Chorus.

4 Saviour, hasten thine appearing;
   Bring, O bring the glorious day!
When, the awful summons hearing,
   Heaven and earth shall pass away!
Then with golden harps we'll sing,
Glory, glory, to our King.

63   7s, D.

The kingdoms of this world are become the kingdoms of our Lord.—REV. 11. 15.

HARK! the song of jubilee,
   Loud as mighty thunders roar,
Or the fulness of the sea,
   When it breaks upon the shore!
Hallelujah! for the Lord
   God omnipotent shall reign!
Hallelujah! let the word
   Echo round the earth and main.

2 Hallelujah! hark, the sound,
   From the depths unto the skies,
Wakes above, beneath, around,
   All creation's harmonies!
See Jehovah's banner furled,
   Sheathed his sword, he speaks—'tis done!
And the kingdoms of this world
   Are the kingdoms of his Son!

3 He shall reign from pole to pole
   With illimitable sway;
He shall reign, when like a scroll
   Yonder heavens are passed away.
Then the end: beneath his rod
   Man's last enemy shall fall:
Hallelujah! Christ in God,
   God in Christ is all in all!

Tabernacle Chorus.

64   8, 7.

*The harvest truly is plenteous.—*MATT. 9. 37.

HARK! the voice of Jesus calling,—
  Who will go and work to-day?
Fields are white, the harvest waiting,
  Who will bear the sheaves away?
Loud and long the Master calleth,
  Rich reward he offers free;
Who will answer, gladly saying,
  Here am I, O Lord, send me.

2 If you cannot cross the ocean
  And the heathen lands explore,
You can find the heathen nearer,
  You can help them at your door.
If you cannot speak like angels,
  If you cannot preach like Paul,
You can tell the love of Jesus,
  You can say he died for all.

3 While the souls of men are dying,
  And the Master calls for you,
Let none hear you idly saying,
  There is nothing I can do!
Gladly take the task he gives you,
  Let his work your pleasure be;
Answer quickly when he calleth,
  Here am I, O Lord, send me.

65   8, 7, 4.

*It is finished.—*JOHN 19. 80.

HARK! the voice of love and mercy
  Sounds aloud from Calvary;

𝕿𝖆𝖇𝖊𝖗𝖓𝖆𝖈𝖑𝖊 𝕮𝖍𝖔𝖗𝖚𝖘.

See, it rends the rocks asunder,
  Shakes the earth, and veils the sky!
    "It is finished!"
Hear the dying Saviour cry.

2 "It is finished!"—O what pleasure
Do these precious words afford!
Heavenly blessings without measure
  Flow to us from Christ the Lord;
    "It is finished!"
Saints, the dying words record.

3 Finished—all the types and shadows
  Of the ceremonial law;
Finished—all that God had promised;
  Death and hell no more shall awe;
    "It is finished!"
Saints, from hence your comforts draw

4 Tune your harps anew, ye seraphs,
  Join to sing the pleasing theme;
All on earth and all in heaven
  Join to praise Immanuel's name;
    Hallelujah!
Glory to the bleeding Lamb.

66   6, 4.

Let us labour therefore to enter into that rest.
HEB. 4. 11.

HASTE, my dull soul, arise,
  Cast off thy care,
Press to thy native skies,
  Mighty in prayer.
Jesus has gone before,
Count all thy troubles o'er,
He who thy burden bore,
  Jesus is there.

Tabernacle Chorus.

2 Soul, for the marriage-feast
   Robe and prepare,
Pureness becomes each guest:
   Jesus is there.
Saints, wave your victory palms,
Chant your celestial psalms;
Bride of the Lamb, thy charms
   O, let us wear!

3 Heaven's bliss is perfect, pure,
   Glory is there;
Heaven's bliss is ever sure,
   Thou art its heir.
What makes its joy complete?
What makes its hymns so sweet?
There our best Friend we'll meet,
   Jesus is there.

67   7s.

The night cometh.—John 9. 4.

HASTEN, sinner, to be wise;
   Stay not for the morrow's sun:
Wisdom if you still despise,
   Harder is it to be won.

2 Hasten mercy to implore;
   Stay not for the morrow's sun;
Lest thy season should be o'er
   Ere this evening's course be run.

3 Hasten, sinner, to return;
   Stay not for the morrow's sun;
Lest thy lamp should cease to burn
   Ere salvation's work is done.

Tabernacle Chorus.

4 Hasten, sinner, to be blest;
   Stay not for the morrow's sun,
Lest perdition thee arrest,
   Ere the morrow is begun.

68   L. M.

As the shadow of a great rock in a weary land.
ISAIAH 32. 2.

HASTE, traveller, haste! the night comes on,
And many a shining hour is gone;
The storm is gathering in the west,
And thou far off from home and rest.

2 The rising tempest sweeps the sky;
The rains descend, the winds are high;
The waters swell, and death and fear
Beset thy path, nor refuge near.

3 O, yet a shelter you may gain,
A covert from the wind and rain;
A hiding-place, a rest, a home,
A refuge from the wrath to come.

4 Then linger not in all the plain;
Flee for thy life; the mountain gain;
Look not behind; make no delay;
O, speed thee, speed thee on thy way!

69   L. M.

I will bring the blind by a way that they knew not.
ISAIAH 42. 16.

HE leadeth me! O blessed thought,
   O words with heavenly comfort fraught,
Whate'er I do, where'er I be,
Still 'tis God's hand that leadeth me!

Tabernacle Chorus.

2 Sometimes 'mid scenes of deepest gloom,
Sometimes where Eden's bowers bloom,
By waters still, o'er troubled sea—
Still 'tis his hand that leadeth me!

3 Lord, I would clasp thy hand in mine,
Nor ever murmur nor repine—
Content whatever lot I see,
Since 'tis my God that leadeth me.

4 And when my task on earth is done,
When, by thy grace, the vict'ry's won,
E'en death's cold wave I will not flee,
Since God through Jordan leadeth me.

70   7s.
These three are one.—1 JOHN 5. 7.

HOLY Father, hear my cry;
  Holy Saviour, bend thine ear;
Holy Spirit, come thou nigh:
  Father, Saviour, Spirit, hear!

2 Father, save me from my sin,
  Saviour, I thy mercy crave;
Gracious Spirit, make me clean·
  Father, Son, and Spirit, save!

3 Father, let me taste thy love;
  Saviour, fill my soul with peace;
Spirit, come my heart to move:
  Father, Son, and Spirit, bless!

4 Father, Son, and Spirit—thou
  One Jehovah, shed abroad
All thy grace within me now:
  Be my Father and my God!

Tabernacle Chorus.

71 7s.

The love of God is shed abroad in our hearts by the Holy Ghost, which is given unto us. —Rom. 5. 5.

HOLY Ghost, with light divine,
Shine upon this heart of mine;
Chase the shades of night away,
Turn my darkness into day.

2 Holy Ghost, with power divine,
Cleanse this guilty heart of mine;
Long hath sin, without control,
Held dominion o'er my soul.

3 Holy Ghost, with joy divine,
Cheer this saddened heart of mine:
Bid my many woes depart,
Heal my wounded, bleeding heart.

4 Holy Spirit, all divine,
Dwell within this heart of mine;
Cast down every idol throne,
Reign supreme,—and reign alone.

72

The Lord of hosts is with us.—Psa. 46. 11.

HO! my comrades, see the signal
Waving in the sky!
Reinforcements now appearing,
Victory is nigh!

CHORUS:
Hold the fort, for I am coming,
Jesus signals still;
Wave the answer back to heaven,—
By thy grace, we will.

Tabernacle Chorus.

2 See the mighty host advancing,
  Satan leading on;
Mighty men around us falling,
  Courage almost gone.

3 Fierce and long the battle rages,
  But our help is near;
Onward comes our great Commander,
  Cheer, my comrades, cheer!

73 11s.
The rock of my strength, and my refuge is in God.
PSA. 62. 7.

HOW firm a foundation, ye saints of the Lord,
Is laid for your faith in his excellent word;
What more can he say than to you he hath said,
You who unto Jesus for refuge have fled.

2 Fear not, I am with thee, O be not dismayed;
I, I am thy God, and will still give thee aid;
I'll strengthen thee, help thee, and cause thee to stand,
Upheld by my righteous, omnipotent hand.

3 When through the deep waters I call thee to go,
The rivers of sorrow shall not overflow;
For I will be with thee, thy troubles to bless,
And sanctify to thee thy deepest distress.

4 When through fiery trials thy pathway shall lie,
My grace, all sufficient, shall be thy supply;
The flame shall not hurt thee; I only design
Thy dross to consume, and thy gold to refine.

Tabernacle Chorus.

The soul that to Jesus has fled for repose,
I will not, I will not desert to his foes;
That soul, though all hell shall endeavour to
    shake,
I'll never,—no, never,—no, never forsake.

74   C. M.

As in Adam all die, even so in Christ shall all be made alive.—1 Cor. 15. 22.

HOW helpless guilty nature lies,
  Unconscious of its load:
The heart unchanged can never rise
  To happiness and God.

2 Can aught beneath a power divine
  The stubborn will subdue?
'Tis thine, Almighty Saviour, thine,
  To form the heart anew.

3 'Tis thine the passions to recall
  And upwards bid them rise;
And make the scales of error fall
  From reason's darkened eyes.

4 To chase the shades of death away,
  And bid the sinner live,
A beam of heaven, a vital ray,
  'Tis thine alone to give.

5 O change these wretched hearts of ours,
  And give them life divine;
Then shall our passions and our powers,
  Almighty Lord, be thine.

Tabernacle Chorus.

75 C. M.

A better country, that is, a heavenly.—HEB. 11. 16.

HOW pleasant thus to dwell below,
   In fellowship of love;
And though we part, 'tis bliss to know
   The good shall meet above.

CHORUS:

O that will be joyful
To meet, to part no more,
On Canaan's happy shore,
And sing the everlasting song
With those who've gone before.

2 Yes, happy thought! when we are free
   From earthly grief and pain,
In heaven we shall each other see,
   And never part again.

3 Then let us each, in strength divine,
   Still walk in wisdom's ways;
That we, with those we love, may join
   In never-ending praise.

76 C. M.

Sin is the trangression of the law.—1 JOHN 3. 4.

HOW sad our state by nature is!
   Our sin, how deep it stains!
And Satan binds our captive minds
   Fast in his slavish chains.

2 But there's a voice of sov'reign grace
   Sounds from the sacred word:
Ho! ye despairing sinners, come,
   And trust upon the Lord.

Tabernacle Chorus.

3 My soul obeys th' Almighty call,
  And runs to this relief:
I would believe thy promise, Lord,
  O! help mine unbelief.

4 To the dear fountain of thy blood,
  Incarnate God, I fly;
Here let me wash my spotted soul
  From crimes of deepest dye.

5 Stretch out thine arm, victorious King,
  My reigning sins subdue:
Drive the old dragon from his seat,
  With all his hellish crew.

6 A guilty, weak, and helpless worm,
  On thy kind arms I fall:
Be thou my Strength and Righteousness,
  My Jesus, and my All!

77   C. M.

Unto you therefore which believe he is precious.
1 PET. 2. 7.

HOW sweet the name of Jesus sounds
  In a believer's ear!
It soothes his sorrows, heals his wounds,
  And drives away his fear.

2 It makes the wounded spirit whole,
  And calms the troubled breast;
'Tis manna to the hungry soul,
  And to the weary, rest.

3 Dear Name, the rock on which I build,
  My shield and hiding-place;
My never-failing treasury, fill'd
  With boundless stores of grace:

Tabernacle Chorus.

4 Jesus, my Shepherd, Saviour, Friend,
   My Prophet, Priest, and King,
My Lord, my Life, my Way, my End,
   Accept the praise I bring.

5 I would thy boundless love proclaim
   With every fleeting breath;
So shall the music of thy name
   Refresh my soul in death.

78   C. M.
An house not made with hands, eternal in the heavens.—2 COR. 5. 1.

I HAVE a home, a glorious home,
   Which Jesus bought for me;
An ever-blessed home of light,
   From sin and sorrow free.

2 My Saviour's blood, his precious blood,
   The blood so freely spilt,
Hath paid the all-availing price—
   The price of all my guilt.

3 My Saviour's love, his dying love,
   Hath made my hope secure,
And, safe in him, I journey on;
   I know my home is sure.

4 His gracious smile, his loving smile,
   Shall cheer me all the way;
The pilgrim road I'll gladly walk
   That leads to glorious day.

5 I'll praise his love, his boundless love,
   His love and grace divine,
By which that happy home's secured,
   Secured, forever mine.

Tabernacle Chorus.

6 His grace divine, his power divine,
    My strength, my hope shall be,
And bear me to my blessed home,
    My Jesus there to see.

79   C. M.

I will give you rest.—MATT. 11. 28.

I HEARD the voice of Jesus say,
    Come unto me and rest;
Lay down, thou weary one, lay down
    Thy head upon my breast.
I came to Jesus as I was,
    Weary, and worn, and sad:
I found in him a resting-place,
    And he has made me glad.

2 I heard the voice of Jesus say,
    Behold, I freely give
The living water; thirsty one,
    Stoop down and drink and live.
I came to Jesus, and I drank
    Of that life-giving stream;
My thirst was quenched, my soul revived
    And now I live in him.

3 I heard the voice of Jesus say
    I am this dark world's light,
Look unto me, thy morn shall rise
    And all thy day be bright.
I looked to Jesus, and I found
    In him my Star, my Sun;
And in that light of life I'll walk,
    Till all my journey's done.

Tabernacle Chorus.

80

Having obtained eternal redemption for us.
HEB. 9. 12.

I HEAR my Saviour say,
  Thy strength indeed is small,
Thou hast naught thy debt to pay,
  Find in me thy all in all.

CHORUS:
Jesus paid it all,
  All to him I owe;
Sin had left a crimson stain,
  He washed it white as snow.

2 Yea, nothing good have I
  Whereby thy grace to claim;
I'll wash my garments white
  In the blood of Calvary's Lamb.

3 And now complete in him,
  My robe his righteousness,
Close sheltered 'neath his side,
  I am divinely blest.

4 When from my dying bed
  My ransomed soul shall rise,
My Jesus paid it all,
  Shall echo through the skies.

5 And when before the throne
  I stand in him complete,
I'll lay my trophies down,
  All down at Jesus' feet.

Tabernacle Chorus.

81   L. M.
I know that my Redeemer liveth.—Job 19. 25.

I KNOW that my Redeemer lives:
  What comfort this sweet sentence gives!
He lives, he lives, who once was dead,
He lives, my ever living head.

2 He lives to bless me with his love,
He lives to plead for me above;
He lives my hungry soul to feed,
He lives to help in time of need.

3 He lives to silence all my fears,
He lives to wipe away my tears;
He lives to calm my troubled heart,
He lives, all blessings to impart.

4 He lives, all glory to his name!
He lives, my Jesus, still the same;
O the sweet joy this sentence gives,
I know that my Redeemer lives!

82   7, 6.
Christ was once offered to bear the sins of many.
Heb. 9. 28.

I LAY my sins on Jesus,
  The spotless Lamb of God;
He bears them all, and frees us
  From the accursed load.
I bring my guilt to Jesus,
  To wash my crimson stains
White, in his blood most precious,
  Till not a spot remains.

Tabernacle Chorus.

2 I lay my wants on Jesus;
  All fulness dwells in him;
He heals all my diseases,
  He doth my soul redeem.
I lay my griefs on Jesus,
  My burdens and my cares;
He from them all releases,
  He all my sorrow shares.

3 I rest my soul on Jesus,
  This weary soul of mine;
His right hand me embraces,
  I on his breast recline.
I love the name of Jesus,
  Immanuel, Christ, the Lord;
Like fragrance on the breezes
  His name abroad is poured.

4 I long to be like Jesus,
  Meek, loving, lowly, mild;
I long to be like Jesus,
  The Father's holy child.
I long to be with Jesus,
  Amid the heavenly throng,
To sing with saints his praises,
  To learn the angels' song.

83

I am a stranger with thee, and a sojourner, as all my fathers were.—Psa. 39. 12.

I'M a pilgrim, and I'm a stranger,
  I can tarry, I can tarry but a night;
Do not detain me, for I am going
To where the fountains are ever flowing
I'm a pilgrim, and I'm a stranger,
  I can tarry, I can tarry but a night.

Tabernacle Chorus.

2 There the glory is ever shining;
I am longing, I am longing for the sight;
Here in this country so dark and dreary,
I have been wand'ring, forlorn and weary;
I'm a pilgrim, and I'm a stranger,
I can tarry, I can tarry but a night.

3 There's the city to which I journey;
My Redeemer, my Redeemer is its light;
There is no sorrow, nor any sighing,
There is no sin there, nor any dying.
I'm a pilgrim, and I'm a stranger,
I can tarry, I can tarry but a night.

84 6, 4.
Strangers and pilgrims on the earth.—HEB. 11. 18.

I'M but a stranger here,
  Heaven is my home;
Earth is a desert drear,
  Heaven is my home;
Dangers and sorrows stand
Round me on every hand,
Heaven is my Fatherland,
  Heaven is my home.

2 What though the tempest rage?
  Heaven is my home;
Short is my pilgrimage,
  Heaven is my home;
And time's wild, wintry blast
Soon will be over-past,
I shall reach home at last—
  Heaven is my home.

Tabernacle Chorus.

3 Therefore I murmur not,
   Heaven is my home;
Whate'er my earthly lot,
   Heaven is my home;
And I shall surely stand
There at my Lord's right hand,
Heaven is my Fatherland—
   Heaven is my home.

85

There remaineth therefore a rest to the people of God.—Heb. 4. 9.

IN the Christian's home in glory
   There remains a land of rest;
There my Saviour's gone before me,
   To fulfil my soul's request.

      Chorus:
   There is rest for the weary,
   There is rest for the weary;
   On the other side of Jordan,
   In the sweet fields of Eden,
   Where the tree of life is blooming,
     There is rest for you!

2 He is fitting up my mansion,
   Which eternally shall stand;
For my stay shall not be transient
   In that holy, happy land.

3 Death itself shall then be vanquished,
   And his sting shall be withdrawn;
Shout for gladness, O ye ransomed!
   Hail with joy the rising morn.

Tabernacle Chorus.

4 Sing, O sing, ye heirs of glory!
   Shout your triumphs as you go;
Zion's gates will open for you,
   You shall find an entrance through.

86   C. M.

The forgiveness of sins, according to the riches of his grace.—Eph. 1. 7.

I SAW One hanging on a tree
   In agony and blood,
Who fixed his languid eyes on me
   As near the cross I stood.

2 Sure never, till my latest breath,
   Can I forget that look;
It seemed to charge me with his death,
   Though not a word he spoke.

3 Alas! I knew not what I did,
   But now my tears are vain;
Where shall my trembling soul be hid,
   For I the Lord have slain!

4 A second look he gave that said,
   I freely all forgive:
This blood is for thy ransom paid;
   I die that thou mayst live.

5 Thus while his death my sin displays
   In all its blackest hue,
Such is the mystery of grace,
   It seals my pardon too!

Tabernacle Chorus.

87   S. M.

Whoso liveth and believeth in me shall never die.
    JOHN 11. 26.

IT is not death to die—
  To leave this weary road,
And 'mid the brotherhood on high,
  To be at home with God.

2 It is not death to close
  The eye long dimmed by tears,
And wake, in glorious repose,
  To spend eternal years.

3 It is not death to bear
  The wrench that sets us free
From dungeon chain to breathe the air
  Of boundless liberty.

4 It is not death to fling
  Aside this sinful dust,
And rise, on strong exulting wing,
  To live among the just.

5 Jesus, thou Prince of life!
  Thy chosen cannot die;
Like thee, they conquer in the strife,
  To reign with thee on high.

88   S. M.

Ye were as sheep going astray; but are now returned unto the shepherd and bishop of your souls.
—1 PETER 2. 25.

I WAS a wand'ring sheep,
  I did not love the fold;
I did not love my Shepherd's voice,
  I would not be controlled.

Tabernacle Chorus.

I was a wayward child,
  I did not love my home,
I did not love my Father's voice,
  I loved afar to roam.

2 The Shepherd sought his sheep,
  The Father sought his child;
They followed me o'er vale and hill,
  O'er deserts waste and wild.
They found me nigh to death,
  Famished, and faint, and lone;
They bound me with the bands of love,
  They saved the wand'ring one.

3 Jesus my Shepherd is,
  'Twas he that loved my soul;
'Twas he that washed me in his blood,
  'Twas he that made me whole.
'Twas he that sought the lost,
  That found the wandering sheep;
'Twas he that brought me to the fold,
  'Tis he that still doth keep.

4 No more a wandering sheep,
  I love to be controlled;
I love my tender Shepherd's voice,
  I love the peaceful fold.
No more a wayward child,
  I seek no more to roam;
I love my heavenly Father's voice,
  I love, I love his home.

89 11s.
I would not live alway.—JOB 7. 16.

I WOULD not live alway: I ask not to stay
  Where storm after storm rises dark o'er the
    way;

Tabernacle Chorus.

The few lurid mornings that dawn on us here
Are enough for life's woes, full enough for its cheer.
2 I would not live alway, thus fettered by sin,
Temptation without, and corruption within;
E'en the rapture of pardon is mingled with fears,
And the cup of thanksgiving with penitent tears.
3 I would not live alway; no, welcome the tomb;
Since Jesus hath lain there, I dread not its gloom:
There sweet be my rest till he bid me arise,
To hail him in triumph descending the skies.
4 Who, who would live alway, away from his God—
Away from yon heaven, that blissful abode,
Where the rivers of pleasure flow o'er the bright plains,
And the noontide of glory eternally reigns?
5 Where the saints of all ages in harmony meet,
Their Saviour and brethren transported to greet;
While the anthems of rapture unceasingly roll,
And the smile of the Lord is the feast of the soul!

90   C. M.
An inheritance incorruptible, undefiled, and that fadeth not away.—1 PETER 1. 4.

JERUSALEM, my happy home,
  Name ever dear to me,

Tabernacle Chorus.

When shall my labours have an end,
  In joy, and peace, and thee?

2 O when, thou city of my God,
  Shall I thy courts ascend,
Where congregations ne'er break up,
  And Sabbaths have no end?

3 There happier bowers than Eden's bloom
  Nor sin, nor sorrow know;
Blest seats! through rude and stormy scenes,
  I onward press to you.

4 Why should I shrink at pain and woe,
  Or feel at death dismay?
I've Canaan's goodly land in view,
  And realms of endless day.

5 Apostles, martyrs, prophets, there
  Around my Saviour stand;
And soon my friends in Christ below
  Will join the glorious band.

6 Jerusalem, my happy home!
  My soul still pants for thee;
Then shall my labours have an end
  When I thy joys shall see.

91   L. M.

Whosoever shall deny me before men, him will I also deny before my Father which is in heaven.— MATT. 10. 33.

JESUS! and can it ever be,
  A mortal man ashamed of thee!
Ashamed of thee, whom angels praise—
Whose glories shine through endless days!

Tabernacle Chorus.

2 Ashamed of Jesus! sooner far
Let evening blush to own a star;
He sheds the beams of light divine
O'er this benighted soul of mine.

3 Ashamed of Jesus! that dear friend
On whom my hopes of heaven depend?
No; when I blush, be this my shame,
That I no more revere his name.

4 Ashamed of Jesus! Yes, I may,
When I've no guilt to wash away,—
No tear to wipe, no good to crave,
No fears to hush, no soul to save.

5 Till then—nor is my boasting vain—
Till then I boast a Saviour slain!
And O may this my glory be,
Jesus is not ashamed of me!

92

I will arise and go to my father.—LUKE 15. 18.

JESUS, I come to thee,
   A wand'rer, a wand'rer;
A stranger from my Father's house
I would no longer be.
Jesus, I plead with thee,
   A wand'rer, a wand'rer;
O wash me in thy cleansing blood,
   And set my spirit free.

CHORUS:
Now, blessed Saviour,
   Take thy weary, wand'ring child,
Keep me, O keep me
   From the tempest wild;

Tabernacle Chorus.

My lonely heart by sin oppress'd
Would lose its burden on thy breast,
And find a calm and peaceful rest,
  Forever there.

2 Jesus, the living way,
  O save me, O save me!
O lead me to thy precious fold,
And let me never stray;
O let me hear thy voice,
  My Father, My Father!
In gentle tones my pardon speak,
And bid my soul rejoice.

3 Jesus, the way is bright,
  Before me, before me;
My prayer is heard, the clouds are gone,
I see the glorious light:
Jesus, no more I'll roam
  A wand'rer, a wand'rer;
My Father holds me in his arms,
And bids me welcome home.

93   7s.

In the shadow of thy wings will I make my refuge.—Psa. 57. 1.

JESUS, lover of my soul,
  Let me to thy bosom fly,
While the billows near me roll,
  While the tempest still is high;
Hide me, O my Saviour, hide,
  Till the storm of life is past;
Safe into the haven guide,
  O receive my soul at last.

Tabernacle Chorus.

2 Other refuge have I none;
   Hangs my helpless soul on thee:
Leave, ah! leave me not alone;
   Still support and comfort me:
All my trust on thee is stayed;
   All my help from thee I bring;
Cover my defenceless head
   With the shadow of thy wing.

3 Plenteous grace with thee is found,—
   Grace to pardon all my sin:
Let the healing streams abound;
   Make and keep me pure within.
Thou of life the fountain art;
   Freely let me take of thee:
Spring thou up within my heart;
   Rise to all eternity.

94   L. M.

*In whom we have boldness and access with confidence by the faith of him.—*Eph. 3. 12.

JESUS, my all, to heaven is gone:
   He whom I fix my hopes upon:
His track I see, and I'll pursue
The narrow way, till him I view.

2 This is the way I long have sought,
And mourned because I found it not;
My grief a burden long has been,
Because I was not saved from sin.

3 The more I strove against its power
I felt its weight and guilt the more;
Till late I heard my Saviour say,
Come hither, soul, I am the way.

Tabernacle Chorus.

4 Lo! glad I come; and thou, blest Lamb.
Shall take me to thee as I am;
Nothing but sin have I to give,
Nothing but love shall I receive.

5 Then will I tell to sinners round
What a dear Saviour I have found;
I'll point to thy redeeming blood,
And say, Behold the way to God.

95 8, 7.
They saw no man, save Jesus only.—MATT. 17. 8.

JESUS only, when the morning
   Beams upon the path I tread;
Jesus only, when the darkness
   Gathers round my weary head.

2 Jesus only, when the billows
   Cold and sullen o'er me roll;
Jesus only, when the trumpet
   Rends the tomb and wakes the soul.

3 Jesus only, when in judgment
   Boding fears my heart appal;
Jesus only, when the wretched
   On the rocks and mountains call.

4 Jesus only, when, adoring,
   Saints their crowns before him bring:
Jesus only, I will, joyous,
   Through eternal ages sing.

96 L. M
Whose dominion is an everlasting dominion, and his kingdom is from generation to generation.—DAN. 4. 3.

JESUS shall reign where'er the sun
   Does his successive journeys run:

Tabernacle Chorus.

His kingdom stretch from shore to shore,
Till suns shall rise, and set no more.

2 To him shall endless prayer be made,
And endless praises crown his head;
His name, like sweet perfume, shall rise
With every morning sacrifice.

3 People and realms of every tongue
Dwell on his love with sweetest song;
And infant voices shall proclaim
Their early blessings on his name.

4 Let every creature rise and bring
Peculiar honours to our King;
Angels descend with songs again,
And earth repeat the loud Amen.

97   6, 4.
We love him, because he first loved us.
1 JOHN 4. 19.

JESUS, thy name I love
  All other names above,
    Jesus, my Lord!
O! thou art all to me!
Nothing to please I see,
Nothing apart from thee,
    Jesus, my Lord!

2 Thou, blessed Son of God,
Hast bought me with thy blood,
    Jesus, my Lord!
O! how supreme thy love,
All other loves above,
Love that I daily prove,
    Jesus, my Lord!

Tabernacle Chorus.

3 When unto thee I flee
Thou wilt my refuge be,
    Jesus, my Lord!
What need I now to fear?
What earthly grief or care,
Since thou art ever near?
    Jesus, my Lord!

4 Soon thou wilt come again,
I shall be happy then,
    Jesus, my Lord!
Then thine own face I'll see,
Then shall I like thee be,
Then evermore with thee,
    Jesus, my Lord?

98   S. M.

Pray without ceasing.—1 THESS. 5. 17.

JESUS, who knows full well
    The heart of every saint,
Invites us all our griefs to tell,
    To pray and never faint.

2 He bows his gracious ear—
    We never plead in vain;
Then let us wait till he appear,
    And pray, and pray again.

3 Jesus, the Lord, will hear
    His chosen when they cry;
Yes, though he may awhile forbear,
    He'll help them from on high.

4 Then let us earnest cry,
    And never faint in prayer;
He sees, he hears, and from on high
    Will make our cause his care.

Tabernacle Chorus.

99   C. M.

A light to lighten the Gentiles, and the glory of thy people Israel.—LUKE 2. 32.

JOY to the world, the Lord is come!
   Let earth receive her King;
Let every heart prepare him room,
   And heaven and nature sing.

2 Joy to the world, the Saviour reigns!
   Let men their songs employ:
While fields and floods, rocks, hills, and plains,
   Repeat the sounding joy.

3 No more let sin and sorrow grow,
   Nor thorns infest the ground;
He comes to make his blessings flow
   Far as the curse is found.

4 He rules the world with truth and grace,
   And makes the nations prove
The glories of his righteousness,
   And wonders of his love.

100   L. M.

And him that cometh to me, I will in no wise cast out.—JOHN 6. 37.

JUST as I am, without one plea
   But that thy blood was shed for me,
And that thou bidd'st me come to thee,
      O Lamb of God, I come!

2 Just as I am, and waiting not
To rid my soul of one dark blot,
To thee, whose blood can cleanse each spot,
      O Lamb of God, I come!

Tabernacle Chorus.

3 Just as I am, though tossed about
With many a conflict, many a doubt,
With fears within and wars without,
    O Lamb of God, I come!

4 Just as I am, poor, wretched, blind,
Sight, riches, healing of the mind,
Yes, all I need, in thee to find,
    O Lamb of God, I come!

5 Just as I am,—thou wilt receive,
Wilt welcome, pardon, cleanse, relieve:
Because thy promise I believe,
    O Lamb of God, I come!

6 Just as I am,—thy love unknown
Has broken every barrier down;
Now to be thine, yea, thine alone,
    O Lamb of God, I come!

101   L. M.
All that the Father giveth me shall come to me.
JOHN 6. 37.

JUST as thou art,—without one trace
  Of love, or joy, or inward grace,
Or meetness for the heavenly place,
    O guilty sinner, come!

2 Thy sins I bore on Calvary's tree,
The stripes thy due were laid on me,
That peace and pardon might be free,—
    O wretched sinner, come!

3 Come, leave thy burden at the cross;
Count all thy gains but empty dross:
My grace repays all earthly loss,—
    O needy sinner, come!

Tabernacle Chorus.

4 Come, hither bring thy boding fears,
Thy aching heart, thy bursting tears;
'Tis mercy's voice salutes thine ears,—
      O trembling sinner, come!

5 The Spirit and the bride say, Come;
Rejoicing saints re-echo, Come;
Who faints, who thirsts, who will, may come:
      Thy Saviour bids thee come.

102   7s.

The Lord of hosts, he is the King of glory.
PSA. 24. 10.

KING of glory, reign in me:
  Bind my willing heart to thee:
Be my Ruler and my Friend;
With thy royal power defend.

2 King of glory, fight for me;
Thine the victory shall be;
In thy majesty divine
Conquer all thy foes and mine.

3 King of glory, praise to thee!
Vanquish all my foes for me,
Victor in the final strife,
King of kings, and Prince of life

103   8, 7

Looking for the coming of the day of God.
2 PET. 3. 12.

LAND a-head! Its fruits are waving
  O'er the hills of fadeless green;
And the living waters laving
  Shores where heavenly forms are seen

Tabernacle Chorus.

CHORUS.
Rocks and storms I'll fear no more,
  When on that eternal shore.
Drop the anchor! Furl the sail!
  I am safe within the vail.

2 Onward, bark! the cape I'm rounding;
  See the blessed wave their hands;
Hear the harps of God resounding
  From the bright immortal bands.

3 There, let go the anchor, riding
  On this calm and silv'ry bay;
Seaward fast the tide is gliding,
  Shores in sunlight stretch away.

4 Now we're safe from all temptation
  All the storms of life are past;
Praise the Rock of our salvation,
  We are safe at home at last.

104   C. P. M.
We shall all stand before the judgment-seat of Christ.—ROM. 14. 10.

LO! on a narrow neck of land,
  'Twixt two unbounded seas I stand,
    Secure! insensible!
A point of time, a moment's space,
Removes me to yon heavenly place,
  Or shuts me up in hell.

2 O God! my inmost soul convert,
And deeply on my thoughtful heart
    Eternal things impress:
Give me to feel their solemn weight,
And save me ere it be too late;
    Wake me to righteousness.

Tabernacle Chorus.

3 Before me place, in dread array,
The pomp of that tremendous day
   When thou with clouds shalt come
To judge the nations at thy bar;
And tell me, Lord! shall I be there
   To meet a joyful doom!

4 Be this my one great business here,—
With holy trembling, holy fear,
   To make my calling sure!
Thine utmost counsel to fulfil,
And suffer all thy righteous will,
   And to the end endure!

5 Then, Saviour, then my soul receive,
Transported from this vale, to live,
   And reign with thee above;
Where faith is sweetly lost in sight,
And hope, in full, supreme delight,
   And everlasting love.

105   8, 7, 4.

Save thy people, and bless thine inheritance: feed them also, and lift them up forever.—PSA. 28. 9.

LORD, dismiss us with thy blessing:
   Fill our hearts with joy and peace,
Let us each, thy love possessing,
   Triumph in redeeming grace;
      O refresh us,
   Travelling through this wilderness.

2 Thanks we give, and adoration
   For the gospel's joyful sound;
May the fruits of thy salvation
   In our hearts and lives abound,
      May thy presence
With us evermore be found.

Tabernacle Chorus.

3 So, whene'er the signal's given
  Us from earth to call away,
Borne on angel's wings to heaven,
  Glad to leave our cumbrous clay,—
    May we, ready,
  Rise and reign in endless day.

106   C. M.

Casting all your care upon him; for he careth for you.
1 Pet. 5. 7.

LORD, it belongs not to my care
  Whether I die or live;
To love and serve thee is my share,
  And this thy grace must give.

2 If life be long, I will be glad
  That I may long obey;
If short, yet why should I be sad
  To soar to endless day?

3 Christ leads me through no darker rooms
  Than he went through before;
No one into his kingdom comes,
  But through his opened door.

4 Come, Lord, when grace has made me meet
  Thy blessed face to see;
For if thy work on earth be sweet,
  What will thy glory be!

5 Then shall I end my sad complaints,
  And weary, sinful days,
And join with all triumphant saints
  Who sing Jehovah's praise.

6 My knowledge of that life is small:
  The eye of faith is dim;
But 't is enough that Christ knows all,
  And I shall be with him.

Tabernacle Chorus.

107 S. M.
What manner of persons ought ye to be?
  2 Pet. 3. 11.

MAKE haste, O man, to live,
  For thou so soon must die;
Time hurries past thee like the breeze;
  How swift its moments fly!

2 To breathe, and wake, and sleep,
  To smile, to sigh, to grieve,
To move in idleness through earth—
  This, this is not to live.

3 Make haste, O man, to do
  Whatever must be done;
Thou hast no time to lose in sloth,
  Thy day will soon be gone.

4 Up, then, with speed, and work;
  Fling ease and self away;
This is no time for thee to sleep—
  Up, watch and work and pray!

108 11s.
I shall be satisfied when I awake with thy likeness.
  Psa. 17. 15.

'MID scenes of confusion and creature complaints,
How sweet to my soul is communion of saints
To find at the banquet of mercy there's room,
And feel in the presence of Jesus at home:
  Home, home, sweet, sweet home,
    Prepare me, dear Saviour, for glory, my home.

Tabernacle Chorus.

2 While here in the valley of conflict I stay,
O give me submission, and strength as my day;
In all my afflictions to thee would I come,
Rejoicing in hope of my own glorious home.

3 Whate'er thou deniest, O give me thy grace!
The Spirit's sure witness, and smiles of thy face;
Endue me with patience to wait at thy throne,
And find even now a sweet foretaste of home.

4 I long, dearest Lord, in thy beauties to shine,—
No more as an exile in sorrow to pine,—
And in thy dear image arise from the tomb,
With glorified millions to praise thee at home.

109

The glorious liberty of the children of God.—ROM. 8. 21.

MINE eyes have seen the glory of the coming of the Lord;
He is tramping out the vintage where the grapes of wrath are stored;
He hath loosed the fateful lightning of his terrible quick sword:
    His truth is marching on.
      CHORUS:
    Glory, glory, hallelujah!
    Glory, glory, hallelujah!
    Glory, glory, hallelujah!
    His truth is marching on.

Tabernacle Chorus.

2 I have seen him in the watchfires of a hundred circling camps;
They have builded him an altar in the evening dews and damps;
I have read his righteous sentence by the dim and flaring lamps:
    His day is marching on.

3 I have read a fiery gospel, writ in burnished rows of steel,
As ye deal with my contemners, so with you my grace shall deal;
Let the Hero, born of woman, crush the serpent with his heel,
    Since God is marching on.

4 He has sounded forth the trumpet that shall never call retreat;
He is sifting out the hearts of men before his judgment-seat:
O be swift, my soul, to answer him! be jubilant, my feet:
    Our God is marching on.

5 In the beauty of the lilies Christ was born across the sea,
With a glory in his bosom that transfigures you and me;
As he died to make men holy, let us die to make men free,
    While God is marching on.

Tabernacle Chorus.

110   6, 4.

*Lovest thou me?—*John 21. 17.

MORE love to thee, O Christ!
  More love to thee!
Hear thou the prayer I make
  On bended knee;
This is my earnest plea,—
More love, O Christ! to thee,
  More love to thee!

2 Once earthly joy I craved,
  Sought peace and rest;
Now thee alone I seek,
  Give what is best:
This all my prayer shall be,—
More love, O Christ! to thee,
  More love to thee!

3 Let sorrow do its work
  Send grief and pain;
Sweet are thy messengers,
  Sweet their refrain,
When they can sing with me,—
More love, O Christ! to thee,
  More love to thee!

4 Then shall my latest breath
  Whisper thy praise;
This be the parting cry
  My heart shall raise,—
This still its prayer shall be,—
More love, O Christ! to thee,
  More love to thee!

Tabernacle Chorus.

111 C. M.
If we suffer, we shall also reign with him.—2 Tim. 2. 12.

MUST Jesus bear the cross alone,
  And all the world go free?
No, there's a cross for every one,
  And there's a cross for me.

2 The consecrated cross I'll bear,
  Till death shall set me free,
And then go home my crown to wear,
  For there's a crown for me.

3 Upon the crystal pavement, down
  At Jesus' piercéd feet,
Joyful, I'll cast my golden crown,
  And his dear name repeat.

4 And palms shall wave, and harps shall ring
  Beneath heaven's arches high,
The Lord that lives, the ransomed sing,
  That lives no more to die.

5 O precious cross! O glorious crown!
  O resurrection day!
Ye angels, from the skies come down,
  And bear my soul away.

112 6, 4,
Where the Spirit of the Lord is, there is liberty.
  2 Cor. 3. 17.

MY country! 'tis of thee,
  Sweet land of liberty,
    Of thee I sing;
Land where my fathers died,
Land of the Pilgrims' pride,
From every mountain's side,
    Let freedom ring.

Tabernacle Chorus.

2 My native country! thee,
Land of the noble free,
   Thy name I love:
I love thy rocks and rills,
Thy woods and templed hills;
My heart with rapture thrills
   Like that above.

3 Our Father's God! to thee,
Author of liberty!
   To thee we sing;
Long may our land be bright
With freedom's holy light;
Protect us by thy might,
   Great God, our King!

113

We rejoice in the hope of the glory of God.—Rom. 5. 2.

MY days are gliding swiftly by,
   And I, a pilgrim stranger,
Would not detain them as they fly,
   Those hours of toil and danger.
      CHORUS:
   For O! we stand on Jordan's strand,
      Our friends are passing over,
   And just before, the shining shore
      We may almost discover.

2 We'll gird our loins, my brethren dear,
   Our heavenly home discerning;
Our absent Lord has left us word,
   Let every lamp be burning

3 Should coming days be cold and dark,
   We need not cease our singing;
That perfect rest naught can molest,
   Where golden harps are ringing.

Tabernacle Chorus.

4 Let sorrow's rudest tempest blow,
 Each chord on earth to sever;
Our King says come, and there's our home,
 Forever, O forever!

114   S. M.

*Let us not sleep, as do others, but let us
watch and be sober.*—1 Thess. 5. 6.

MY soul, be on thy guard;
 Ten thousand foes arise;
And hosts of sin are pressing hard,
 To draw thee from the skies.

2 O watch, and fight, and pray;
 The battle ne'er give o'er;
Renew it boldly every day,
 And help divine implore.

3 Ne'er think the vict'ry won,
 Nor once at ease sit down;
Thine arduous work will not be done
 Till thou hast got thy crown.

4 Fight on, my soul, till death
 Shall bring thee to thy God;
He'll take thee at thy parting breath,
 Up to his blest abode.

115   6, 4.

*In thee, O Lord, do I put my trust; let me
never be put to confusion.*—Psa. 71. 1.

MY faith looks up to thee
 Thou Lamb of Calvary;
 Saviour divine,

Tabernacle Chorus.

Now hear me while I pray;
Take all my guilt away;
O let me from this day
  Be wholly thine.

2 May thy rich grace impart
Strength to my fainting heart;
  My zeal inspire:
As thou hast died for me,
O may my love to thee
Pure, warm, and changeless be—
  A living fire

3 While life's dark maze I tread,
And griefs around me spread,
  Be thou my Guide:
Bid darkness turn to day;
Wipe sorrow's tears away,
Nor let me ever stray
  From thee aside.

4 When ends life's transient dream;
When death's cold, sullen stream
  Shall o'er me roll;
Blest Saviour, then, in love,
Fear and distrust remove:
O bear me safe above,
  A ransom'd soul.

116

Behold, I stand at the door, and knock.—Rev. 3. 20.

MY Saviour stands waiting, and knocks at the door,
  Has knocked, and is knocking again;
I hear his kind voice; I'll reject him no more,
  Nor let him stand pleading in vain.

Tabernacle Chorus.

In infinite mercy he came from above
  To ransom, to cleanse me from sin;
I'll yield to the voice of his merciful love,
  And let my dear Saviour come in.

    CHORUS:

  Saviour, come in;
  Cleanse me from sin;
Jesus, my Saviour, come in, come in!
    Enter the door,
    Waiting no more;
Saviour, dear Saviour, come in.

2 O Saviour, my Ransom, Redeemer, and Friend,
  The Life, and the Truth, and the Way,
On thy precious merit alone I depend;
  Dwell in me and keep me. I pray.
Thy goodness hath opened the door of my heart;
  'Tis open in welcome to thee;
Come in, blessed Saviour, and never depart;
  Come in, with thy mercy, to me.

117   6, 4.

Draw nigh to God, and he will draw nigh to you.—JAMES 4. 8.

NEARER, my God, to thee,—
  Nearer to thee!
E'en though it be a cross
  That raiseth me;
Still all my song shall be,
Nearer, my God, to thee,
  Nearer to thee!

Tabernacle Chorus.

2 Though like a wanderer,
    The sun gone down,
Darkness comes over me,
    My rest a stone,
Yet in my dreams I'd be
Nearer, my God, to thee,
    Nearer to thee!

3 There let my way appear
    Steps unto heaven;
All that thou sendest me
    In mercy given;
Angels to beckon me
Nearer, my God, to thee,
    Nearer to thee!

4 Then with my waking thoughts
    Bright with thy praise,
Out of my stony griefs
    Bethel I'll raise:
So by my woes to be
Nearer, my God, to thee,
    Nearer to thee!

5 And when on joyful wing,
    Cleaving the sky,
Sun, moon, and stars forgot,
    Upward I fly;
Still all my song shall be,
Nearer, my God, to thee,
    Nearer to thee!

Tabernacle Chorus.

118 (*Woodland.*) C. M.

*Through the grace of our Lord Jesus Christ,
we shall be saved.*—Acts 15. 11.

NO merit of my own I bring
  Before my Maker's face,
For in me dwelleth no good thing;
My only plea before the King—
  A sinner saved by grace.

2 My poor, weak heart is full of sin,
  In thought and word and deed;
Yet He who died my soul to win,
In mercy bids me enter in,
  And pities all my need.

3 He is my blessed Advocate;
  He paid my debt for me;
And while on him in faith I wait,
He opens wide the heavenly gate
  With welcome, COME TO ME!

4 O Saviour, Christ, on thee I call:
  In faith I bring to thee
My load of sins, both great and small;
Thy precious blood can cleanse them all;
  Thy blood can set me free.

119 7s

*Let us make a joyful noise to the rock of
our salvation.*—Psa. 95. 1.

NOW begin the heavenly theme;
  Sing aloud in Jesus' name;
Ye, who his salvation prove,
Triumph in redeeming love.

Tabernacle Chorus.

2 Ye who see the Father's grace
Beaming in the Saviour's face,
As to Canaan on ye move,
Praise and bless redeeming love.

3 Mourning souls, dry up your tears,
Banish all your guilty fears;
See your guilt and curse remove,
Canceled by redeeming love.

4 Ye, alas! who long have been
Willing slaves of death and sin,
Now from bliss no longer rove,
Stop, and taste redeeming love.

5 Welcome, all by sin oppressed,
Welcome to his sacred rest:
Nothing brought him from above,
Nothing,—but redeeming love.

6 Hither, then, your music bring,
Strike aloud each joyful string;
Mortals, join the hosts above,
Join to praise redeeming love.

120   6, 4.
Who shall separate us from the love of Christ?
Rom. 8. 35.

NOW I have found a Friend
  Whose love shall never end;
    Jesus is mine.
Though earthly joys decrease,
Though human friendships cease,
Now I have lasting peace;
    Jesus is mine.

Tabernacle Chorus.

2 Though I grow poor and old,
He will my faith uphold;
 Jesus is mine.
He shall my wants supply;
His precious blood is nigh;
Naught can my hope destroy;
 Jesus is mine.

3 When earth shall pass away,
In the great judgment day,
 Jesus is mine.
O what a glorious thing
Then to behold my King,
On tuneful harps to sing,
 Jesus is mine!

4 Father! thy name I bless;
Thine was the sov'reign grace;
 Praise shall be thine;
Spirit of holiness!
Sealing the Father's grace,
Thou mad'st my soul embrace
 Jesus as mine.

121   S. M.

Behold, now is the accepted time; behold, now is the day of salvation.—2 Cor. 6. 2.

NOW is the accepted time;
 Now is the day of grace;
Now, sinners, come without delay,
 And seek the Saviour's face.

2 Now is the accepted time;
 The Saviour calls to-day;
To-morrow it may be too late,—
 Then why should you delay?

Tabernacle Chorus.

3 Now is the accepted time;
   The Gospel bids you come;
And every promise in his word
   Declares there yet is room.

4 Lord, draw reluctant souls,
   And feast them with thy love;
Then will the angels swiftly fly,
   And bear the news above.

122   C. M.

Understandest thou what thou readest?
ACTS 8. 30.

O BLESSED message from on high!
   O word of truth and grace,
That brings the hope of endless life
   To all our ransomed race!
O priceless pearl of living joy!
   O treasury of delight
That shows, in rich, almighty love,
   My Saviour to my sight!

2 O word that pierces thickest clouds,
   That cheers the darkest night,
That lifts upon the gloomiest path
   Its lamp of life and light!
That speaks of pardon and of peace
   To mortals in despair,
And tells the poor desponding soul
   That God will hear his prayer.

3 O word that tells my Father's love,
   The love that from on high
Brought down the sinless Son of God
   For guilty man to die!

Tabernacle Chorus.

Open my eyes, O Holy Ghost,
  And help me to behold
The wondrous treasures of thy word,
  More precious far than gold.

123   C. P. M.

Unto you therefore which believe he is precious.
1 PET. 2. 7.

O COULD I speak the matchless worth,
  O could I sound the glories forth,
    Which in my Saviour shine!
I'd soar, and touch the heavenly strings,
And vie with Gabriel while he sings
    In notes almost divine.

2 I'd sing the precious blood he spilt,
My ransom from the dreadful guilt
    Of sin and wrath divine!
I'd sing his glorious righteousness,
In which all-perfect, heavenly dress
    My soul shall ever shine.

3 I'd sing the characters he bears,
And all the forms of love he wears,
    Exalted on his throne:
In loftiest songs of sweetest praise,
I would to everlasting days
    Make all his glories known.

4 Well—the delightful day will come
When my dear Lord will bring me home,
    And I shall see his face:
Then with my Saviour, Brother, Friend,
A blest eternity I'll spend,
    Triumphant in his grace.

Tabernacle Chorus.

124   L. M.
Choose you this day whom ye will serve.
JOSH. 24. 15.

O DO not let the word depart,
   And close thine eyes against the light;
Poor sinner, harden not thy heart;
   Thou would'st be saved—Why not to-night?

2 To-morrow's sun may never rise
   To bless thy long-deluded sight;
This is the time! O then be wise!
   Thou would'st be saved—Why not to-night?

3 The world has nothing left to give—
   It has no new, no pure delight;
O try the life which Christians live!
   Thou would'st be saved—Why not to-night?

4 Our God in pity lingers still,
   And wilt thou thus his love requite?
Renounce at length thy stubborn will;
   Thou would'st be saved—Why not to-night?

5 Our blessed Lord refuses none
   Who would to him their souls unite;
Then be the work of grace begun!
   Thou would'st be saved—Why not to-night?

125   C. M.
That shineth more and more unto the perfect day.
PROV. 4. 18.

O FOR a closer walk with God,—
   A higher, holier frame;
A brighter light upon the road
   That leads me to the Lamb!

Tabernacle Chorus.

2 Rich blessedness e'en now I know,
  In converse with the Lord;
Soul-quickening views are granted me
  Of Jesus and his word.

3 But there are lengths and breadths of love
  My spirit would attain,—
Deep things of God that I would search,
  Heights that I long to gain.

4 And I would have this soul of mine
  Made "glorious within,"
Adorned with grace, meet for my Lord!
  And sure his smile to win.

5 The work is thine, O holy Dove!
  I gladly welcome thee;
Come in, blest Spirit of the Lord!
  Possess both mine and me.

6 How close is now my walk with God!
  How glad my upward way!
Brighter and brighter shines the light
  Unto the perfect day.

126   C. M.
Let every thing that hath breath praise the Lord.
Psa. 150. 6.

O FOR a thousand tongues to sing
  My great Reedeemer's praise,—
The glories of my God and King,
  The triumphs of his grace!

2 My gracious Master and my God,
  Assist me to proclaim,
To spread through all the earth abroad
  The honours of thy name.

Tabernacle Chorus.

3 Jesus! the name that calms our fears,
   That bids our sorrows cease;
'Tis music in the sinner's ears;
   'Tis life, and health, and peace.

4 Look unto him, ye nations; own
   Your God, ye fallen race;
Look, and be saved through faith alone,
   Be justified by grace.

127   L. M.

Thy vows are upon me, O God: I will render praises unto thee.—Psa. 56. 12.

O HAPPY day, that stays my choice
   On thee, my Saviour and my God;
Well may this glowing heart rejoice,
   And tell thy goodness all abroad.

Chorus.

Happy day, happy day,
When Jesus washed my sins away;
He taught me how to watch and pray,
And live rejoicing every day.

2 O happy bond, that seals my vows,
   To Him who merits all my love;
Let cheerful anthems fill his house,
   While to his sacred throne I move.

3 'Tis done, the great transaction's done;
   Deign, gracious Lord, to make me thine;
Help me through grace to follow on,
   Glad to confess thy voice divine.

Tabernacle Chorus.

4 Here rest, my oft divided heart;
   Fixed on thy God, thy Saviour, rest;
Who with the world would grieve to part
   When called on angels' food to feast?

5 High heaven, that heard the solemn vow,
   That vow renewed shall daily hear,
Till in life's latest hour I bow,
   And bless in death a bond so dear.

128   C. M.

*To him that overcometh will I give to eat of
the tree of life.*—Rev. 2. 7.

ON Jordan's stormy banks I stand,
   And cast a wishful eye
To Canaan's fair and happy land,
   Where my possessions lie.

2 O the transporting, rapturous scene
   That rises to my sight!
Sweet fields arrayed in living green,
   And rivers of delight.

3 O'er all those wide extended plains
   Shines one eternal day;
There God the Son forever reigns,
   And scatters night away.

4 When shall I reach that happy place,
   And be forever blest?
When shall I see my Father's face,
   And in his bosom rest?

Tabernacle Chorus.

129   C. M.
Put on the whole armour of God.—EPH. 6. 11.

O SPEED thee, Christian, on thy way,
  And to thine armour cling;
With girded loins the call obey,
  The call of Christ, thy King.

2 There is a battle to be fought,
  An upward race to run,
A crown of glory to be sought,
  A vict'ry to be won.

3 O faint not, Christian! for thy sighs
  Are heard before the throne;
The race must come before the prize,
  The cross before the crown.

130   L. M.
Thou canst make me clean.—MARK 1. 40.

O THAT my load of sin were gone;
  O that I could at last submit
At Jesus' feet to lay it down,
  To lay my soul at Jesus' feet!

2 Rest for my soul I long to find;
  Saviour of all, if mine thou art,
Give me thy meek and lowly mind,
  And stamp thine image on my heart.

3 Break off the yoke of inbred sin,
  And fully set my spirit free;
I cannot rest till pure within,
  Till I am wholly lost in thee.

Tabernacle Chorus.

4 Fain would I learn of thee, my God;
    Thy light and easy burden prove;
The cross, all stained with hallow'd blood,
    The labour of thy dying love.

5 I would, but thou must give the power,
    My heart from every sin release;
Bring near, bring near the joyful hour,
    And fill me with thy perfect peace.

131   L. M.

Wash me thoroughly from my iniquity, and cleanse me from my sin.—Psa. 51. 2.

O THOU that hear'st when sinners cry,
    Though all my crimes before thee lie,
Behold them not with angry look,
But blot their memory from thy book.

2 Though I have grieved thy spirit, Lord,
Thy help and comfort still afford;
And let a wretch come near thy throne,
To plead the merits of thy Son.

3 A broken heart, my God, my King,
Is all the sacrifice I bring;
The God of grace will ne'er despise
A broken heart for sacrifice.

132   C. M.

Comfort ye, comfort ye my people, saith your God.
Isa. 40. 1.

O THOU who driest the mourner's tear!
    How dark this world would be,
If, when deceived and wounded here,
    We could not fly to thee!

Tabernacle Chorus.

2 When joy no longer soothes or cheers,
   And e'en the hope that threw
A moment's sparkle o'er our tears
   Is dimmed and vanished too;—

3 O, who would bear life's stormy doom,
   Did not thy wing of love
Come, brightly wafting through the gloom,
   Our peace-branch from above?

4 Then sorrow, touch'd by thee, grows bright,
   With more than rapture's ray;
As darkness shows us worlds of light
   We never saw by day.

133   C. M.

God over all, blessed forever.—Rom. 9. 5.

OUR God, our help in ages past,
   Our hope for years to come,
Our shelter from the stormy blast,
   And our eternal home!

2 Before the hills in order stood,
   Or earth received her frame,
From everlasting thou art God,
   To endless years the same.

3 Time, like an ever-rolling stream,
   Bears all its sons away;
They fly, forgotten, as a dream
   Dies at the op'ning day.

4 Our God, our help in ages past,
   Our hope for years to come,
Be thou our guard while troubles last,
   And our eternal home.

Tabernacle Chorus.

134

For I reckon that the sufferings of the present time are not worthy to be compared with the glory which shall be revealed in us.—Rom. 8. 18.

OUT on an ocean all boundless we ride,
 We're homeward bound, homeward bound;
Tossed on the waves of a rough, restless tide,
 We're homeward bound, homeward bound.
Far from the safe, quiet harbour we've rode,
Seeking our Father's celestial abode,
Promise of which on us each he bestowed,
 We're homeward bound, homeward bound.

2 Wildly the storm sweeps us on as it roars,
 We're homeward bound.
Look! yonder lie the bright heavenly shores,
 We're homeward bound.
Steady, O pilot, stand firm at the wheel;
Steady! we soon shall outweather the gale,
O how we fly 'neath the loud creaking sail!
 We're homeward bound.

3 Into the harbour of heaven now we glide,
 We're home at last.
Softly we drift on its bright silver tide.
 We're home at last.
Glory to God! all our dangers are o'er;
We stand secure on the glorified shore,
Glory to God! we will shout evermore.
 We're home at last.

Tabernacle Chorus.

135   C. M.
Unto you therefore which believe he is precious.
1 Pet. 2. 7.

O WHAT hath Jesus done for me!
   He died to save my soul;
My sins were great, his mercy free;
   His blood hath made me whole.

CHORUS:
He shed his precious blood for me,
He gave his precious life for me,
The Saviour in glory pleads for me,
   And bids me welcome home,
   Welcome home.

2 He helpeth me in time of need
   By his almighty grace;
For me he evermore doth plead,
   And I shall see his face.

3 Exalted at the Father's side,
   My mansion he prepares;
My home of glory he'll provide;
   He answers all my prayers.

4 He is my Lord, my risen Friend—
   He reigns upon the throne;
And he will keep me to the end,
   Through faith in him alone.

136   S. M.
And I saw the dead, small and great, stand before God.—Rev. 20. 12.

O WHERE shall rest be found—
   Rest for the weary soul?
'Twere vain the ocean's depths to sound,
   Or pierce to either pole.

Tabernacle Chorus.

2 The world can never give
   The bliss for which we sigh:
'Tis not the whole of life to live,
   Nor all of death to die.

3 Beyond this vale of tears
   There is a life above,
Unmeasur'd by the flight of years;
   And all that life is love.

4 There is a death whose pang
   Outlasts the fleeting breath:
O what eternal horrors hang
   Around the second death!

5 Lord God of truth and grace,
   Teach us that death to shun:
Lest we be banished from thy face,
   And evermore undone.

137   6, 5.

O magnify the Lord with me, and let us exalt his name together.—PSA. 34. 8.

O WORSHIP the King
   All-glorious above;
O gratefully sing
   His power and his love!
Our Shield and Defender,
   The Ancient of Days,
Pavilioned in splendour,
   And girded with praise.

2 O tell of his might!
   O sing of his grace!
Whose robe is the light,
   Whose canopy space!

Tabernacle Chorus.

His chariots of wrath
    The deep thunder-clouds form,
And dark is his path
    On the wings of the storm.

3 Thy bountiful care
    What tongue can recite?
It breathes in the air,
    It shines in the light,
It streams from the hills,
    It descends to the plains,
And sweetly distils
    In the dew and the rains.

4 Frail children of dust,
    And feeble as frail,
In thee do we trust,
    Nor find thee to fail;
Thy mercies how tender!
    How firm to the end!
Our Maker, Defender,
    Redeemer, and Friend.

138   7s.

*Salvation to our God which sitteth upon the throne and unto the Lamb.—*Rev. 7. 10.

PALMS of glory, raiment bright,
    Crowns that never fade away,
Gird and deck the saints in light,
    Priests, and kings, and conq'rors they.

2 Yet the conq'rors bring their palms
    To the Lamb amidst the throne,
And proclaim in joyful psalms,
    Victory through his cross alone.

Tabernacle Chorus.

3 Kings for harps their crowns resign,
   Crying, as they strike the chords,
Take the kingdom, it is thine,
   King of kings, and Lord of lords!

4 Round the altar priests confess,
   If their robes are white as snow,
'Twas the Saviour's righteousness,
   And his blood, that made them so.

5 Who are these?—on earth they dwelt,
   Sinners once of Adam's race;
Guilt and fear and suff'ring felt,
   But were saved by sov'reign grace.

6 They were mortal too, like us:
   Ah! when we, like them, shall die,
May our souls, translated thus,
   Triumph, reign, and shine on high.

139

Jesus, thou Son of David, have mercy on me.
LUKE 18. 38.

PASS me not, O gentle Saviour,
   Hear my humble cry;
While on others thou art calling,
   Do not pass me by.

CHORUS:

Saviour, Saviour,
   Hear my humble cry;
While on others thou art smiling,
   Do not pass me by.

Tabernacle Chorus.

2 Let me at thy throne of mercy
   Find a sweet relief;
Kneeling there in deep contrition,
   Help my unbelief.

3 Trusting only in thy merits,
   Would I seek thy face;
Heal my wounded, broken spirit,
   Save me by thy grace.

4 Thou the spring of all my comfort,
   More than life to me,
Whom have I on earth beside thee,
   Whom in heaven but thee.

140   L. M.

Therefore being justified by faith, we have peace with God through our Lord Jesus Christ.—Rom. 5. 1.

PEACE, troubled soul, whose plaintive moan
  Hath taught each scene the note of woe;
Cease thy complaint, suppress thy groan,
  And let thy tears forget to flow:
Behold, thy precious balm is found,
To lull thy pain, and heal thy wound.

2 Come, freely come, by sin opprest,
   On Jesus cast thy weighty load;
In him thy refuge find, thy rest,
   Safe in the mercy of thy God:
Thy God's thy Saviour, glorious word:
O hear, believe, and bless the Lord.

Tabernacle Chorus.

141 C. M.

Christ Jesus came into the world to save sinners.
1 Tim. 1. 15.

PLUNGED in a gulf of dark despair,
  We wretched sinners lay,
Without one cheerful beam of hope,
  Or spark of glimm'ring day.

2 With pitying eyes the Prince of grace
  Beheld our helpless grief;
He saw, and O! amazing love!
  He ran to our relief.

3 Down from the shining seats above
  With joyful haste he fled,
Entered the grave in mortal flesh,
  And dwelt among the dead.

4 O for this love, let rocks and hills
  Their lasting silence break,
And all harmonious human tongues
  The Saviour's praises speak.

142 L. M.

The Father, the Word, and the Holy Ghost: and these
three are one.—1 John 5. 7.

PRAISE God, from whom all blessings flow;
  Praise him, all creatures here below;
Praise him above, ye heavenly host;
Praise Father, Son, and Holy Ghost.

Tabernacle Chorus

143 C. M.

Lord, teach us to pray.—LUKE 11. 1.

PRAYER is the soul's sincere desire,
   Uttered or unexpressed;
The motion of a hidden fire
   That trembles in the breast.

2 Prayer is the burden of a sigh,
   The falling of a tear;
The upward glancing of an eye
   When none but God is near.

3 Prayer is the simplest form of speech,
   That infant lips can try;
Prayer the sublimest strains that reach
   The Majesty on high.

4 Prayer is the Christian's vital breath,
   The Christian's native air:
His watchword at the gates of death—
   He enters heaven with prayer.

5 Prayer is the contrite sinner's voice,
   Returning from his ways;
While angels in their songs rejoice,
   And cry—Behold, he prays!

6 O thou, by whom we come to God—
   The Life, the Truth, the Way;
The path of prayer thyself hast trod;
   Lord! teach us how to pray.

Tabernacle Chorus.

144   C. M.

And the times of this ignorance God winked at; but now commandeth all men every where to repent. Acts 17. 30.

REPENT! the voice celestial cries,
  Nor longer dare delay:
The soul that scorns the mandate dies,
  And meets a fiery day.

2 No more the sov'reign eye of God
  O'erlooks the crimes of men;
His heralds now are sent abroad
  To warn the world of sin.

3 O sinners! in his presence bow,
  And all your guilt confess;
Accept the offered Saviour now,
  Nor trifle with his grace.

4 Soon will the awful trumpet sound,
  And call you to his bar;
His mercy knows th' appointed bound,
  And yields to justice there.

5 Amazing love—that yet will call,
  And yet prolong our days!
Our hearts, subdued by goodness, fall,
  And weep, and love, and praise.

145   L. M.

Return unto the Lord, and he will have mercy.
    Isa. 55. 7.

RETURN, O wanderer, return,
  And seek an injured Father's face;
Those warm desires that in thee burn
  Were kindled by reclaiming grace.

Tabernacle Chorus.

2 Return, O wanderer, return,
  And seek a Father's melting heart;
His pitying eyes thy grief discern,
  His hand shall heal thy inward smart.

3 Return, O wanderer, return,
  Thy Saviour bids thy spirit live;
Go to his bleeding feet, and learn
  How freely Jesus can forgive.

4 Return, O wanderer, return,
  And wipe away the falling tear;
'Tis God who says, No longer mourn;
  'Tis Mercy's voice invites thee near.

146   7, 6.

The world passeth away, and the lust thereof, but he that doeth the will of God abideth forever.—1 JOHN 2. 17.

RISE, my soul, and stretch thy wings
  Thy better portion trace;
Rise from transitory things
  Toward heaven, thy native place.
Sun, and moon, and stars decay,
  Time shall soon this earth remove;
Rise, my soul, and haste away
  To seats prepared above.

2 Rivers to the ocean run,
  Nor stay in all their course;
Fire, ascending, seeks the sun,
  Both speed them to their source.
So the soul that's born of God
  Pants to see his glorious face,
Upward tends to his abode,
  To rest in his embrace.

Tabernacle Chorus.

3 Cease, ye pilgrims, cease to mourn;
   Press onward to the prize;
Soon our Saviour will return,
   Triumphant, in the skies.
Yet a season, and you know
   Happy entrance will be given;
All our sorrows left below,
   And earth exchanged for heaven

147   7s.

Thou art the rock of my salvation.—PSA. 89. 26.
And that rock was Christ.—1 COR. 10. 4.

ROCK of ages, cleft for me,
   Let me hide myself in thee;
Let the water and the blood,
From thy side a healing flood,
Be of sin the double cure,—
Save from wrath and make me pure.

2 Should my tears forever flow,
Should my zeal no langour know,
This for sin could not atone;
Thou must save, and thou alone:
In my hand no price I bring;
Simply to thy cross I cling.

3 While I draw this fleeting breath,
When my eyelids close in death,
When I rise to worlds unknown,
And behold thee on thy throne,—
Rock of ages, cleft for me,
Let me hide myself in thee.

Tabernacle Chorus.

148   7s.

Ye shall keep my sabbaths, and reverence my sanctuary.—LEV. 26. 2.

SAFELY through another week
  God has brought us on our way;
Let us now a blessing seek,
  Waiting in his courts to-day;
Day of all the week the best,
Emblem of eternal rest.

2 While we seek supplies of grace,
  Through the dear Redeemer's name,
Show thy reconciling face,
  Take away our sin and shame;
From our worldly cares set free,
May we rest this day in thee.

3 May the Gospel's joyful sound
  Conquer sinners, comfort saints,
Make the fruits of grace abound,
  Bring relief from all complaints:
Thus let all our Sabbaths prove,
Till we join the Church above.

149   C. M.

I will joy in the God of my salvation.
HAB. 3. 18.

SALVATION! O the joyful sound,
  Glad tidings to our ears;
A sov'reign balm for every wound,
  A cordial for our fears.

2 Salvation! buried once in sin,
  At hell's dark door we lay;
But now we rise by grace divine,
  And see a heavenly day.

Tabernacle Chorus.

3 Salvation! O thou bleeding Lamb,
 To thee the praise belongs:
Salvation shall inspire our hearts,
 And dwell upon our tongues.

4. Salvation! let the echo fly
 The spacious earth around;
While all the armies of the sky
 Conspire to raise the sound.

150   6, 4.

I will bring the blind by a way that they knew not.—Isa. 42. 16.

SAVIOUR! I follow on,
 Guided by thee,
Seeing not yet the hand
 That leadeth me.
Hushed be my heart and still,
Fear I no further ill;
Only to meet thy will
 My will shall be.

2 Often to Marah's brink
 Have I been brought;
Shrinking the cup to drink,
 Help I have sought;
And with the prayer's ascent,
Jesus the branch hath rent,
Quickly relief hath sent,
 Sweet'ning the draught.

3 Saviour! I long to walk
 Closer with thee;
Led by thy guiding hand,
 Ever to be;

Tabernacle Chorus.

Constantly near thy side,
Quickened and purified,
Living for him who died
Freely for me!

151   7s.

Jesus, the author and finisher of our faith.
HEB. 12. 2.

SAVIOUR, PROPHET, PRIEST, and KING,
Unto thee glad praise I sing;
Humbled once, for me to die;
Now enthroned above the sky.

2 Saviour, PROPHET, Priest, and King,
Unto thee my prayers I bring;
Speak thy word of grace to me;
With thy pardon set me free

3 Saviour, PRIEST at God's right hand,
Mediator, thou dost stand,
Interceding there for me:
Life and hope I find in thee.

4 Saviour, ever reigning KING,
Unto thee my heart I bring.
Praise and glory unto thee,
Gracious King, forever be.

152   8, 7.

O Lord, revive thy work.—HAB. 3. 2.

SAVIOUR, visit thy plantation;
Grant us, Lord, a gracious rain:
All will come to desolation
Unless thou return again.

Tabernacle Chorus.

2 Keep no longer at a distance;—
 Shine upon us from on high,
Lest, for want of thine assistance,
 Every plant should droop and die.

3 Let our mutual love be fervent,
 Make us prevalent in prayers;
Let each one, esteemed thy servant,
 Shun the world's enticing snares.

4 Break the tempter's fatal power;
 Turn the stony heart to flesh;
And begin, from this good hour,
 To revive thy work afresh.

153   P. M.
Lord, what wilt thou have me to do?
Acts 9. 6.

SAVIOUR! thy dying love
 Thou gavest me,
Nor should I aught withhold,
 Dear Lord, from thee;
In love my soul would bow,
My heart fulfil its vow,
Some offering bring thee now,
 Something for thee.

2 At the blest mercy-seat,
 Pleading for me,
My feeble faith looks up,
 Jesus, to thee:
Help me the cross to bear,
Thy wondrous love declare,
Some song to raise, or prayer,
 Something for thee.

Tabernacle Chorus.

3 Give me a faithful heart—
    Likeness to thee—
That each departing day
    Henceforth may see
Some work of love begun,
Some deed of kindness done,
Some wanderer sought and won,
    Something for thee.

154   L. M.
My Spirit shall not always strive with man.
Gen. 6. 3.

SAY, sinner, hath a voice within
    Oft whispered to thy secret soul,
Urged thee to leave the ways of sin,
    And yield thy heart to God's control?

2 Sinner! it was a heavenly voice,—
    It was the Spirit's gracious call;
It bade thee make the better choice,
    And haste to seek in Christ thine all.

3 Spurn not the call to life and light;
    Regard, in time, the warning kind;
That call thou may'st not always slight,
    And yet the gate of mercy find.

4 God's Spirit will not always strive
    With hardened, self-destroying man:
Ye who persist his love to grieve
    May never hear his voice again.

5 Sinner! perhaps, this very day,
    Thy last accepted time may be:
O shouldst thou grieve him now away,
    Then hope may never beam on thee.

Tabernacle Chorus.

155 L. M.

I acknowledge my transgressions: and my sin is ever before me.—Psa. 51. 3.

SHOW pity, Lord, O Lord, forgive;
Let a repenting rebel live.
Are not thy mercies large and free?
May not a sinner trust in thee?

2 O wash my soul from every sin,
And make my guilty conscience clean;
Here on my heart the burden lies,
And past offences pain my eyes.

3 My lips with shame my sins confess,
Against thy law, against thy grace;
Lord, should thy judgments grow severe,
I am condemn'd, but thou art clear.

4 Should sudden vengeance seize my breath,
I must pronounce thee just in death;
And if my soul were sent to hell,
Thy righteous law approves it well.

5 Yet save a trembling sinner, Lord,
Whose hope, still hov'ring round thy word,
Would light on some sweet promise there,
Some sure support against despair.

156 7s.

Redeeming the time, because the days are evil.
Eph. 5. 16.

SINNER, rouse thee from thy sleep;
Wake, and o'er thy folly weep;
Raise thy spirit dark and dead,
Jesus waits his light to shed.

Tabernacle Chorus.

2 Wake from sleep, arise from death,
See the bright and living path:
Watchful tread that path; be wise,
Leave thy folly, seek the skies.

3 Leave thy folly, cease from crime,
From this hour redeem thy time;
Life secure without delay,
Evil is the mortal day.

4 Be not blind and foolish still;
Called of Jesus, learn his will:
Jesus calls from death and night,
Jesus waits to shed his light.

157 7s.
Turn ye from your evil ways; for why will ye die?—Ezek. 33. 11.

SINNERS, turn; why will ye die?
God, your Maker, asks you why?
God, who did your being give,
Made you with himself to live;
He the fatal cause demands,
Asks the work of his own hands,—
Why, ye thankless creatures, why
Will ye cross his love, and die?

2 Sinners, turn; why will ye die?
God, your Saviour, asks you why?
He, who did your souls retrieve,
Died himself, that ye might live.
Will ye let him die in vain?
Crucify your Lord again?
Why, ye ransom'd sinners, why
Will ye slight his grace, and die?

Tabernacle Chorus.

3 Sinners, turn; why will ye die?
God, the Spirit, asks you why?
He, who all your lives hath strove,
Urged you to embrace his love:
Will ye not his grace receive?
Will ye still refuse to live?
O ye dying sinners, why,
Why will ye forever die?

158   S. M.

Take unto you the whole armour of God, that ye may be able to withstand in the evil day, and having done all, to stand.—Eph. 6. 13.

SOLDIERS of Christ, arise,
  And put your armour on,
Strong in the strength which God supplies
  Through his eternal Son;

2 Strong in the Lord of Hosts,
  And in his mighty power,
Who in the strength of Jesus trusts
  Is more than conqueror.

3 Stand then in his great might,
  With all his strength endued;
And take, to arm you for the fight,
  The panoply of God:

4 That having all things done,
  And all your conflicts past,
Ye may o'ercome, through Christ alone,
  And stand complete at last.

Tabernacle Chorus.

159   L. M.

Let your conversation be as becometh the Gospel.—Phil. 1. 27.

SO let our lips and lives express
  The holy Gospel we profess;
So let our works and virtues shine,
To prove the doctrine all divine.

2 Thus shall we best proclaim abroad
The honours of our Saviour God
When his salvation reigns within,
And grace subdues the power of sin.

3 Our flesh and sense must be denied,
Passion and envy, lust and pride;
While justice, temperance, truth and love,
Our inward piety approve.

4 Religion bears our spirits up,
While we expect that blessed hope,
The bright appearance of the Lord,
And faith stands leaning on his word.

160   L. M.

We rejoice in the hope of the glory of God.
Rom. 5. 2.

STAND up, my soul, shake off thy fears,
  And gird the Gospel armour on;
March to the gates of endless joy,
  Where Jesus, thy great Captain's gone.

2 Hell and thy sins resist thy course;
  But hell and sin are vanquished foes;
Thy Saviour nailed them to the cross,
  And sung the triumph when he rose.

Tabernacle Chorus.

3 Then let my soul march boldly on,
    Press forward to the heavenly gate;
There peace and joy eternal reign,
    And glittering robes for conq'rors wait.

4 There shall I wear a starry crown,
    And triumph in Almighty grace,
While all the armies of the skies
    Join in my glorious Leader's praise.

161

That ye may be able to withstand in the evil day, and having done all, to stand.—EPH. 6. 13.

STAND up for Jesus, Christian, stand!
    Firm as a rock on ocean's strand!
Beat back the waves of sin that roll,
Like raging floods, around thy soul!

CHORUS:
    Stand up for Jesus, nobly stand!
    Firm as a rock on ocean's strand!
    Stand up, his righteous cause defend;
    Stand up for Jesus, your best Friend.

2 Stand up for Jesus, Christian, stand!
Sound forth his name o'er sea and land!
Spread ye his glorious word abroad,
Till all the world shall own him Lord!

3 Stand up for Jesus, Christian, stand!
Lift high the cross with steadfast hand!
Till heathen hosts before it fall,
And hail the Saviour Lord of all.

4 Stand up for Jesus, Christian, stand!
Soon with the blest immortal band
We'll dwell for aye, life's journey o'er,
In realms of light on heaven's bright shore.

Tabernacle Chorus.

162   7, 6.

Stand, therefore.—Eph. 6. 14.

STAND up!—stand up for Jesus!
  Ye soldiers of the cross;
Lift high his royal banner,
  It must not suffer loss:
From vict'ry unto vict'ry
  His army shall be led,
Till every foe is vanquish'd,
  And Christ is Lord indeed.

2 Stand up!—stand up for Jesus!
  The trumpet call obey;
Forth to the mighty conflict
  In this his glorious day:
Ye that are men, now serve him
  Against unnumber'd foes;
Your courage rise with danger,
  And strength to strength oppose.

3 Stand up!—stand up for Jesus!
  Stand in his strength alone;
The arm of flesh will fail you—
  Ye dare not trust your own:
Put on the Gospel armour,
  And, watching unto prayer,
Where duty calls, or danger,
  Be never wanting there.

4 Stand up!—stand up for Jesus!
  The strife will not be long;
This day the noise of battle,
  The next the victor's song:

Tabernacle Chorus.

To him that overcometh,
  A crown of life shall be ;
He with the King of Glory
  Shall reign eternally !

163   L. M.

*Cast me not away from thy presence; and take not thy Holy Spirit from me.—*Psa. 51. 11.

STAY, thou insulted Spirit, stay,
  Though I have done thee such despite,
Nor cast the sinner quite away,
  Nor take thine everlasting flight.

2 Though I have most unfaithful been,
  Of all who e'er thy grace received;
Ten thousand times thy goodness seen,
  Ten thousand times thy goodness grieved;

3 Yet O, the chief of sinners spare,
  In honour of my great High-priest!
Nor in thy righteous anger swear
  I shall not see thy people's rest.

4 E'en now my weary soul release,
  And raise me by thy gracious hand;
Guide me into thy perfect peace.
  And bring me to the promised land.

164   L. M.

*Behold, he that keepeth Israel shall neither slumber nor sleep.—*Psa. 121. 4.

SUN of my soul! thou Saviour dear,
  It is not night if thou be near :
O, may no earth-born cloud arise
  To hide thee from thy servant's eyes.

Tabernacle Chorus.

2 When the soft dews of kindly sleep
My wearied eyelids gently steep,
Be my last thought, how sweet to rest
Forever on my Saviour's breast!

3 Abide with me from morn till eve,
For without thee I cannot live;
Abide with me when night is nigh,
For without thee I dare not die.

4 Come near to bless me when I wake,
Ere through the world my way I take;
Abide with me till in thy love
I lose myself in heaven above.

165   L. M.

Unto thee, O Lord, do I lift up my soul.—PSA. 86. 4.

SWEET hour of prayer, sweet hour of prayer,
That calls me from a world of care,
And bids me at my Father's throne
Make all my wants and wishes known:
In seasons of distress and grief
My soul has often found relief,
And oft escaped the tempter's snare,
By thy return, sweet hour of prayer.

2 Sweet hour of prayer, sweet hour of prayer,
Thy wings shall my petition bear
To Him whose truth and faithfulness
Engage the waiting soul to bless:
And since he bids me seek his face,
Believe his word, and trust his grace,
I'll cast on him my every care,
And wait for thee, sweet hour of prayer.

Tabernacle Chorus.

3 Sweet hour of prayer, sweet hour of prayer,
May I thy consolation share;
Till, from Mount Pisgah's lofty height,
I view my home, and take my flight:
This robe of flesh I'll drop, and rise
To seize the everlasting prize;
And shout, while passing through the air,
Farewell, farewell, sweet hour of prayer.

166   7, 6, 8.

And so shall we ever be with the Lord.
1 Thess. 4. 17.

TEN thousand times ten thousand,
   In sparkling raiment bright,
The armies of the ransomed saints
   Throng up the steeps of light:
'Tis finished, all is finished,
   Their fight with death and sin
Fling open wide the golden gates
   And let the victors in.

2 What rush of hallelujahs
   Fills all the earth and sky!
What ringing of a thousand harps
   Bespeaks the triumph nigh!
O day for which creation
   And all its tribes were made!
O joy, for all its former woes
   A thousand fold repaid!

3 O then what raptured greetings
   On Canaan's happy shore,
What knitting severed friendships up,
   Where partings are no more!

Tabernacle Chorus.

Then eyes with joy shall sparkle
  That brimmed with tears of late;
Orphans no longer fatherless,
  Nor widows desolate.

167   C. M.

He bowed the heavens also, and came down: and darkness was under his feet.—Psa. 18. 9.

THE Lord descended from above
  And bowed the heavens most high;
And underneath his feet he cast
  The darkness of the sky.

2 On cherubim and seraphim
  Full royally he rode,
And on the wings of mighty winds
  Came flying all abroad.

3 And like a den most dark he made
  His hid and secret place;
With waters dark and thickest clouds
  He veiled his glorious face.

4 He sat serene upon the floods,
  Their fury to restrain;
And he, as sov'reign Lord and King,
  For evermore shall reign.

168

The Lord reigneth, he is clothed with majesty.
Psa. 98. 1.

THE Lord Jehovah reigns,
  His throne is built on high,
The garments he assumes
  Are light and majesty;
His glories shine with beams so bright,
No mortal eye can bear the sight.

Tabernacle Chorus.

2 The thunders of his hand
    Keep the wide world in awe;
  His wrath and justice stand,
    To guard his holy law;
And where his love resolves to bless,
His truth confirms and seals the grace.

3 Through all his perfect work
    Surprising wisdom shines;
  Confounds the powers of hell,
    And breaks their curs'd designs:
Strong is the arm—and shall fulfil
His great decrees, his sov'reign will.

4 And can this mighty King
    Of glory condescend—
  And will he write his name,
    My Father and my Friend?
I love his name, I love his word;
Join, all my powers, and praise the Lord!

169   L. M.
The Lord cometh, with ten thousand of his saints.
JUDE 14.

THE Lord shall come! the earth shall quake;
  The mountains to their centre shake;
And withering from the vault of night,
The stars withdraw their feeble light.

2 The Lord shall come! but not the same
As once in lowly form he came,—
A silent Lamb before his foes,
A weary Man, and full of woes.

3 The Lord shall come! a dreadful form,
With wreath of flame, and robe of storm,
On cherub-wings, and wings of wind,
Anointed Judge of human kind!

Tabernacle Chorus.

4 Can this be he, who, wont to stray
A pilgrim on the world's highway,
By power oppress'd, and mocked by pride,
The Nazarene, the crucified?

5 While sinners in despair shall call,
Rocks, hide us! mountains, on us fall!
The saints, ascending from the tomb,
Shall sing for joy, The Lord is come!

170   7, 6.
The earth shall be full of the knowledge of the Lord.—Isa. 11. 9.

THE morning light is breaking,
  The darkness disappears;
The sons of earth are waking
  To penitential tears:
Each breeze that sweeps the ocean
  Brings tidings from afar,
Of nations in commotion,
  Prepared for Zion's war.

2 See heathen nations bending
  Before the God we love,
And thousand hearts ascending
  In gratitude above;
While sinners now confessing,
  The Gospel call obey,
And seek the Saviour's blessing,—
  A nation in a day.

3 Bless'd river of salvation,
  Pursue thy onward way;
Flow thou to every nation,
  Nor in thy richness stay;

Tabernacle Chorus.

Stay not till all the lowly
    Triumphant reach their home;
Stay not till all the holy
    Proclaim—The Lord is come!

171   C. M.

Being now justified by his blood, we shall be saved from wrath through him.—Rom. 5. 9.

THERE is a fountain, filled with blood,
    Drawn from Immanuel's veins,
And sinners plunged beneath that flood
    Lose all their guilty stains.

2 The dying thief rejoiced to see
    That fountain in his day;
And there may I, as vile as he,
    Wash all my sins away.

3 Dear dying Lamb, thy precious blood
    Shall never lose its power,
Till all the ransomed Church of God
    Be saved, to sin no more.

4 E'er since, by faith, I saw the stream
    Thy flowing wounds supply,
Redeeming love has been my theme,
    And shall be till I die.

5 Then, in a nobler, sweeter song,
    I'll sing thy power to save;
When this poor lisping, stamm'ring tongue
    Lies silent in the grave.

Tabernacle Chorus.

172.   C. M.

At thy right hand there are pleasures for evermore.—Psa. 16. 11.

THERE is a land of pure delight,
  Where saints immortal reign;
Eternal day excludes the night,
  And pleasures banish pain.

2 There everlasting spring abides,
  And never-fading flowers.
Death, like a narrow sea, divides
  This heavenly land from ours.

3 Bright fields beyond the swelling food
  Stand dress'd in living green;
So to the Jews fair Canaan stood,
  While Jordan roll'd between.

4 But timorous mortals start, and shrink
  To cross the narrow sea;
And linger, trembling, on the brink,
  And fear to launch away.

5 O, could we make our doubts remove,
  Those gloomy doubts that rise,
And see the Canaan that we love,
  With faith's illumined eyes;—

6 Could we but climb where Moses stood,
  And view the landscape o'er,
Not Jordan's stream, nor death's cold flood,
  Should fright us from the shore.

Tabernacle Chorus.

173   C. M

A name which is above every name.—PHIL. 2. 9.

THERE is a name I love to hear;
  I love to speak its worth:
It sounds like music in mine ear,
  The sweetest name on earth.

2 It tells me of a Saviour's love,
  Who died to set me free;
It tells me of his precious blood,
  The sinner's perfect plea.

3 Jesus! the name I love so well,
  The name I love to hear!
No saint on earth its worth can tell,
  No heart conceive how dear.

4 His name shall shed its fragrance still
  Along this stormy road,
Shall sweetly smooth the rugged hill
  That leads me up to God.

5 And there, with all the blood-bought throng,
  From sin and sorrow free,
I'll sing the new eternal song
  Of Jesus' love for me.

174   S. M.

And whosoever will, let him take the water of life freely.—REV. 22. 17.

THE Spirit in our hearts
  Is whispering, sinner, come!
The bride, the Church of Christ, proclaims
  To all his children, Come!

Tabernacle Chorus.

2 Let him that heareth say
   To all about him, Come!
Let him that thirsts for righteousness,
   To Christ, the Fountain, come!

3 Yes, whosoever will,
   O let him freely come,
And freely drink the stream of life!
   'Tis Jesus bids him come.

4 Lo! Jesus, who invites,
   Declares, I quickly come!
Lord, even so! I wait thy hour:
   Jesus, my Saviour, come!

175   L. M.

There remaineth therefore a rest to the people of God.—HEB. 4. 9.

THINE earthly Sabbaths, Lord, we love,
   But there's a nobler rest above;
To that our weary souls aspire
With ardent pangs of strong desire.

2 No more fatigue, no more distress,
Nor sin, nor death, shall reach the place,
No groans shall mingle with the songs
Which warble from immortal tongues.

3 No rude alarms of raging foes;
No cares to break the long repose;
No midnight shade, no clouded sun,-
But sacred, high, eternal noon.

4 O long-expected day, begin!
Dawn on these realms of woe and sin:
Fain would we leave this weary road,
And sleep in death, to rest with God.

Tabernacle Chorus.

176   8, 7.

The glory of God did lighten it, and the Lamb is the light thereof.—REV. 21. 23.

THIS is not my place of resting—
  Mine's a city yet to come;
Onward to it I am hasting—
  On to my eternal home.

2 In it all is light and glory;
  O'er it shines a nightless day;
Every trace of sin's sad story,
  All the curse, hath pass'd away.

3 There the Lamb, our Shepherd, leads us,
  By the streams of life along;
On the freshest pastures feeds us,
  Turns our sighing into song.

4 Soon we pass this desert dreary,
  Soon we bid farewell to pain;
Nevermore are sad and weary,
  Never, never sin again.

177

He that hath ears to hear, let him hear.
MARK 4. 9.

TO-DAY the Saviour calls,
  Ye wanderers, come!
O, ye benighted souls,
  Why longer roam?

2 To-day the Saviour calls!
  For refuge fly;
The storm of vengeance falls,
  Ruin is nigh.

Tabernacle Chorus.

3 To-day the Saviour calls!
   O, listen now!
Within these sacred walls
   To Jesus bow.

4 The Spirit calls to-day!
   Yield to his power.
O, grieve him not away!
   'Tis mercy's hour.

178   7, 6.

Jesus Christ, and him crucified.—1 Cor. 2. 2.

VAIN, delusive world, adieu,
   With all of creature good;
Only Jesus I pursue,
   Who bought me with his blood.
All thy pleasures I forego,
   All thy wealth, and all thy pride;
Only Jesus will I know,
   And Jesus crucified.

2 Him to know is life and peace,
   And pleasure without end,
This is all my happiness,
   On Jesus to depend:
Daily in his grace to grow,
   And ever in his love abide;
Only Jesus will I know,
   And Jesus crucified.

3 O that I could all invite,
   This saving truth to prove;
Show the length, the breadth, the height,
   And depth of Jesus' love·

Tabernacle Chorus.

Fain I would to sinners show
   His blood by faith alone applied;
Only Jesus will I know,
   And Jesus crucified.

179   7s.

As thy days, so shall thy strength be.
DEUT. 33. 25.

WAIT, my soul, upon the Lord;
   To his gracious promise flee;
Laying hold upon this word,—
   As thy days, thy strength shall be.

2 If the sorrows of thy case
   Seems peculiar still to thee,
God has promised needful grace,—
   As thy days, thy strength shall be.

3 Days of trial, days of grief,
   In succession thou may'st see;
This is still my sweet relief,—
   As thy days, thy strength shall be.

4 Rock of ages, I'm secure,
   With thy promise, full and free,
Faithful, positive, and sure;—
   As thy days, thy strength shall be

180   C. M.

For ye were sometimes darkness, but now are ye light in the Lord.—EPH. 5. 8.

WALK in the light! so shalt thou know
   That fellowship of love,
His Spirit only can bestow
   Who reigns in light above.

Tabernacle Chorus.

2 Walk in the light! and thou shalt find
   Thy heart made truly his,
Who dwells in cloudless light enshrined;
   In whom no darkness is.

3 Walk in the light! and e'en the tomb
   No fearful shade shall wear;
Glory shall chase away its gloom,
   For Christ hath conquer'd there.

4 Walk in the light! and thou shalt see
   Thy path, though thorny, bright;
For God by grace shall dwell in thee,
   And God himself is light.

181   7s.

Surely he hath borne our griefs, and carried our sorrows.—ISA. 53. 4.

WEARY sinner! keep thine eyes
   On th' atoning Sacrifice;
View him bleeding on the tree,
Pouring out his life for thee.

2 Surely Christ thy griefs hath borne;
Weeping soul, no longer mourn;
Now by faith the Son embrace,
Plead his promise, trust his grace.

3 Cast thy guilty soul on him;
Find him mighty to redeem:
At his feet thy burden lay;
Look thy doubts and care away.

4 Lord, come thou with power to heal;
Now thy mighty arm reveal:
At thy feet myself I lay;
Take, O take my sins away!

Tabernacle Chorus.

182 S. M.
A delight, the holy of the Lord, honourable.
Isa. 58. 13.

WELCOME, sweet day of rest,
  That saw the Lord arise,
Welcome to this reviving breast,
  And these rejoicing eyes!

2 The King himself comes near,
  And feasts his saints to-day;
Here we may sit, and see him here,
  And love, and praise, and pray.

3 One day amidst the place
  Where my dear God hath been,
Is sweeter than ten thousand days
  Of pleasurable sin.

4 My willing soul would stay
  In such a frame as this,
And sit and sing herself away
  To everlasting bliss.

183 8, 7, 4.
My son, give me thine heart.—Prov. 23. 26.

WELCOME, welcome, dear Redeemer!
  Welcome to this heart of m'ne;
Lord! I make a full surrender;
  Every power and thought be thine;
    Thine entirely,—
Through eternal ages thine.

Tabernacle Chorus.

2 Known to all to be thy mansion,
　Earth and hell will disappear;
Or in vain attempt possession
　When they find the Lord is near:—
　　Shout, O Zion!
Shout, ye saints! the Lord is here.

184

To him be glory and dominion for ever and ever.
REV. 1. 6.

WE praise thee, O God! for the Son of **thy** love,
For Jesus who died, and is now gone above.

CHORUS:

Hallelujah! thine the glory, Hallelujah! Amen.
Hallelujah! thine the glory, revive us again.

2 We praise thee, O God! for thy Spirit of light,
Who has shown us our Saviour, and scattered our night.

3 All glory and praise to the Lamb that was slain,
Who has borne all our sins, and has cleansed every stain.

4 All glory and praise to the God of all grace,
Who has bought us, and sought us, and guided our ways.

5 Revive us again; fill each heart with thy love;
May each soul be rekindled with fire from above.

Tabernacle Chorus.

185

Be strong in the Lord, and in the power of his might.—EPH. 6. 10.

WE'VE listed in a holy war,
   Battling for the Lord!
Eternal life, our guiding star,
   Battling for the Lord!

CHORUS:

We'll work till Jesus comes,
We'll work till Jesus comes,
We'll work till Jesus comes,
And then we'll rest at home.

2 We've girded on our armour bright,
   Battling for the Lord!
Our Captain's word our strength and might,
   Battling for the Lord!

3 We'll stand like heroes on the field,
   Battling for the Lord!
And in his strength we'll never yield,
   Battling for the Lord!

4 Though sin and death our way oppose,
   Battling for the Lord!
Through grace we'll conquer all our foes,
   Battling for the Lord!

5 And when our glorious war is o'er,
   Conqu'rors through the Lord!
We'll shout salvation evermore,
   Conqu'rors through the Lord!

Tabernacle Chorus.

186   C. M.

I will sing aloud of thy mercy.—Psa. 59. 16.

WHEN all thy mercies, O my God!
   My rising soul surveys,
Transported with the view, I'm lost
   In wonder, love, and praise.

2 Ten thousand thousand precious gifts
   My daily thanks employ;
Nor is the least a cheerful heart
   That tastes those gifts with joy.

3 Through every period of my life
   Thy goodness I'll pursue;
And after death, in distant worlds,
   The glorious theme renew.

4 Through all eternity, to thee
   A joyful song I'll raise:
But O! eternity's too short
   To utter all thy praise!

187   L. M.

Consider the Apostle and High Priest of our profession, Christ Jesus.—Heb. 3. 1.

WHEN gath'ring clouds around I view,
   And days are dark and friends are few
On Him I lean, who, not in vain,
Experienc'd every human pain.
He sees my wants, allays my fears,
And counts and treasures up my tears.

2 If aught should tempt my soul to stray
From heavenly virtue's narrow way,
To fly the good I should pursue,
Or do the sin I should not do;

Tabernacle Chorus.

Still he, who felt temptation's power,
Shall guard me in that dangerous hour.

3 And O, when I have safely past
Through every conflict but the last,
Still, still unchanging, watch beside
My bed of death, for thou hast died;
Then point to realms of cloudless day,
And wipe the latest tear away.

188   C. M.

The gift of God is eternal life through Jesus
Christ our Lord.—Rom. 6. 23.

WHEN I can read my title clear
    To mansions in the skies,
I'll bid farewell to every fear,
    And wipe my weeping eyes.

2 Should earth against my soul engage,
    And fiery darts be hurl'd,
Then I can smile at Satan's rage
    And face a frowning world.

3 Let cares like a wild deluge come,
    And storms of sorrow fall;
May I but safely reach my home,
    My God, my heaven, my all.

4 There shall I bathe my weary soul
    In seas of heavenly rest,
And not a wave of trouble roll
    Across my peaceful breast.

Tabernacle Chorus.

189 L. M.

*We have seen his star in the east.—*Matt. 2. 2.

WHEN, marshall'd on the nightly plain,
   The glittering host bestud the sky,
One star alone, of all the train,
   Can fix the sinner's wand'ring eye.

2 Hark! hark! to God the chorus breaks
   From every host, from every gem;
But one alone the Saviour speaks,
   It is the Star of Bethlehem.

3 Once on the raging seas I rode,
   The storm was loud, the night was dark;
The ocean yawn'd, and rudely blow'd
   The wind that toss'd my found'ring bark.

4 Deep horror then my vitals froze;
   Death-struck, I ceas'd the tide to stem;
When suddenly a star arose,
   It was the Star of Bethlehem!

5 It was my Guide, my Light, my All;
   It bade my dark forebodings cease;
And, through the storm and danger's thrall,
   It led me to the port of peace.

6 Now, safely moor'd, my perils o'er,
   I'll sing, first in night's diadem,
Forever, and for evermore,
   The Star, the Star of Bethlehem!

Tabernacle Chorus.

190　　　　　　　　　　L. M.

Come unto me, all ye that labour and are heavy laden, and I will give you rest.—MATT. 11. 28.

WITH tearful eyes I look around,
　　Life seems a dark and stormy sea;
Yet 'midst the gloom I hear a sound,
　　A heavenly whisper, Come to me.

2 It tells me of a place of rest,—
　　'Tt tells me where my soul may flee;
O, to the weary, faint, oppress'd,
　　How sweet the bidding, Come to me.

3 When nature shudders, loth to part
　　From all I love, enjoy, and see;
When a faint chill steals o'er my heart,
　　A sweet voice utters, Come to me.

4 Come, for all else must fail and die;
　　Earth is no resting-place for thee;
Heavenward direct thy weeping eye;
　　I am thy portion; Come to me.

191　　　　　　　　　　C. P. M.

And he shall set the sheep on his right hand, but the goats on the left.—MATT. 25. 33.

WHEN thou, my righteous Judge, shalt come
To take thy ransom'd people home,
　　Shall I among them stand?
Shall such a worthless worm as I,
Who sometimes am afraid to die,
　　Be found at thy right hand?

Tabernacle Chorus.

2 I love to meet thy people now,
Before thy feet with them to bow,
  Though vilest of them all;
But can I bear the piercing thought,
What if my name should be left out
  When thou for them shalt call?

3 O Lord, prevent it by thy grace,
Be thou my only hiding-place,
  In this the accepted day;
Thy pard'ning voice, O let me hear,
To still my unbelieving fear,
  Nor let me fall, I pray.

4 Among thy saints let me be found
Whene'er th' archangel's trump shall sound,
  To see thy smiling face;
Then loudest of the throng I'll sing,
While heaven's resounding mansions ring
  With shouts of sov'reign grace.

192 L. M.
Shall the dead arise and praise thee?—Psa. 88. 10.

WHILE life prolongs its precious light,
  Mercy is found, and peace is given;
But soon, ah! soon, approaching night
  Shall blot out every hope of heaven.

2 While God invites, how blest the day!
  How sweet the Gospel's charming sound
Come, sinners, haste, O haste away,
  While yet a pard'ning God is found.

3 Soon, borne on time's most rapid wing,
  Shall death command you to the grave,
Before his bar your spirits bring,
  And none be found to hear or save.

Tabernacle Chorus.

4 In that lone land of deep despair
  No Sabbath's heavenly light shall rise;
No God regard your bitter prayer,
  Nor Saviour call you to the skies.

5 Now God invites—how blest the day!
  How sweet the Gospel's charming sound!
Come, sinners, haste. O haste away,
  While yet a pard'ning God is found.

193   7s.

These are they which came out of great tribulation, and have washed their robes, and made them white in the blood of the Lamb.—REV. 7. 14.

WHO are these in bright array,
  This innumerable throng,
Round the altar night and day
  Hymning one triumphant song?
Worthy is the Lamb once slain,
  Blessing, honour, glory, power,
Wisdom, riches, to obtain;
  New dominion every hour.

2 These through fiery trials trod;
  These from great affliction came;
Now before the throne of God,
  Sealed with his eternal name:
Clad in raiment pure and white,
  Victor palms in every hand,
Through their great Redeemer's might,
  More than conquerors they stand.

3 Hunger, thirst, disease, unknown,
  On immortal fruits they feed;
Them the Lamb amidst the throne
  Shall to living fountains lead.

Tabernacle Chorus.

Joy and gladness banish sighs;
  Perfect love dispels their fears;
And forever from their eyes
  God shall wipe away their tears.

194   L. M.
That good part which shall not be taken away.
LUKE 10. 42.

WHY will ye waste on trifling cares
  That life which God's compassion spares?
While, in the various range of thought,
The one thing needful is forgot?

2 Shall God invite you from above?
Shall Jesus urge his dying love?
Shall troubled conscience give you pain?
And all these pleas unite in vain?

3 Not so your eyes will always view
Those objects which you now pursue:
Not so will heaven and hell appear
When death's decisive hour is near.

4 Almighty God! thy grace impart;
Fix deep conviction on each heart;
Nor let us waste on trifling cares
That life which thy compassion spares

195   L. M.
Serve the Lord with gladness: come before his presence with singing.—PSA. 100. 2.

WITH one consent let all the earth
  To God their cheerful voices raise;
Glad homage pay with awful mirth,
  And sing before him songs of praise.

Tabernacle Chorus.

2 Convinced that he is God alone,
   From whom both we and all proceed;
We, whom he chooses for his own,
   The flock that he vouchsafes to feed.

3 O enter, then, his temple gate,
   Thence to his courts devoutly press,
And still your grateful hymns repeat,
   And still his Name with praises bless.

4 For he's the Lord, supremely good,
   His mercy is forever sure:
His truth, which always firmly stood,
   To endless ages shall endure.

196   H. M.
In due season we shall reap, if we faint not.
   GAL. 6. 9.

WORK, Christian labourer, work
   Now while 'tis called to-day,
Toil in thy Master's work,
   And, toiling, watch and pray.
The tempter bids thee pause and sleep;
Work! if thou wouldst the harvest reap.

2 Pray, Christian pilgrim, pray!
   And keep thine armour bright,
Though rugged be the way,
   Though cheerless be the night.
Through darkest night and weariest day
Pray without ceasing—Christian! pray.

3 Fight, Christian soldier, fight!
   The battle is the Lord's;
Strong in Jehovah's might,
   The strength himself affords.
O'er foes without, and foes within,
Strong in the Lord, the day thou'lt win.

Tabernacle Chorus.

4 Wait, Christian workman, wait!
   Nor yet impatient be,
In this thine earthly state,
   The harvest time to see.
The Lord's appointed time will come:
He'll take his faithful workmen home.

197   7, 6.
The night cometh, when no man can work.
      JOHN 9. 4.

WORK, for the night is coming,
   Work through the morning hours;
Work, while the dew is sparkling,
   Work 'mid springing flowers.
Work when the day grows brighter,
   Work in the glowing sun;
Work, for the night is coming,
   When man's work is done.

2 Work, for the night is coming,
   Work through the sunny noon;
Fill brightest hours with labour,
   Rest comes sure and soon;
Give every flying minute
   Something to keep in store;
Work, for the night is coming,
   When man works no more.

3 Work, for the night is coming,
   Under the sunset skies;
While their bright tints are glowing,
   Work, for daylight flies.
Work till the last beam fadeth,
   Fadeth to shine no more;
Work while the night is dark'ning,
   When man's work is o'er.

Tabernacle Chorus.

198 5. 6

They shall speak of the glory of thy kingdom, and talk of thy power.—Psa. 145. 11.

YE servants of God
  Your master proclaim,
And publish abroad
  His wonderful name:
The name all victorious
  Of Jesus extol;
His kingdom is glorious;
  He rules over all.

2 God ruleth on high,
  Almighty to save;
And still he is nigh;
  His presence we have.
The great congregation
  His triumph shall sing,
Ascribing salvation
  To Jesus our King.

3 Then let us adore
  And give him his right,
All glory and power,
  And wisdom and might;
All honour and blessing
  With angels above,
And thanks never ceasing,
  And infinite love.

199 S. M.

Now is our salvation nearer than when we believed.
Rom. 13. 11.

YOUR harps, ye trembling saints,
  Down from the willows take:
Loud to the praise of love divine
  Bid every string awake.

Tabernacle Chorus.

2 Though in a foreign land,
　We are not far from home;
And nearer to our house above
　We every moment come.

3 His grace will to the end
　Stronger and brighter shine;
Nor present things, nor things to come,
　Shall quench the spark divine.

4 When we in darkness walk,
　Nor feel the heavenly flame.
Then is the time to trust our God,
　And rest upon his name.

5 Soon shall our doubts and fears
　Subside at his control;
His loving-kindness shall break through
　The midnight of the soul.

6 Blest is the man, O Lord,
　Who stays himself on thee!
Who waits for thy salvation, Lord,
　Shall thy salvation see.

200

　Glory be to the Father, and to the Son,
　　and to the Holy Ghost.
　As it was in the beginning, is now, and
　　ever shall be,
　World without end.　Amen.

Trinity Supplement.

201   8s & 6s.

AROUND the throne of God in heaven,
   Thousands of Christians stand,
Christians whose sins are all forgiven,
   A holy, happy band,
      Singing glory, glory,
      Glory be to God on high.

2 In flowing robes of spotless white
   See every one arrayed,
Dwelling in everlasting light,
   And joys that cannot fade.

3 What brought them to that world above,
   That heaven so bright and fair,
Where all is peace, and joy, and love,
   How came those Christians there?

4 Because the Saviour shed his blood
   To wash away their sin;
Cleansed by that pure and precious flood,
   Behold them white and clean.

5 On earth they sought the Saviour's grace,
   On earth they loved his name;
So now they see him face to face,
   And stand before the Lamb.

Trinity Supplement.

202   6s & 4s. Peculiar.

CHILD of sin and sorrow,
　Filled with dismay,
Wait not for to-morrow,
　Yield thee to-day;
Heaven bids thee come
While yet there's room,
　　Child of sin and sorrow,
　　　Hear and obey.

2 Child of sin and sorrow,
　Why wilt thou die?
Come, while thou canst borrow
　Help from on high!
Grieve not that love,
Which from above—
　　Child of sin and sorrow—
　　　Would bring thee nigh.

3 Child of sin and sorrow
　Where wilt thou flee?
Through that long to-morrow
　Eternity!
Exiled from home,
Darkly to roam—
　　Child of sin and sorrow,
　　　Where wilt thou flee?

4 Child of sin and sorrow,
　Lift up thine eye!
Heirship thou canst borrow
　In worlds on high!
In that high home,
Graven thy name:
　　Child of sin and sorrow,
　　　Swift homeward fly!

Trinity Supplement.

203 C. M.

COME, every soul by sin oppressed,
  There's mercy with the Lord,
And he will surely give you rest,
  By trusting in his word.

CHORUS.—Only trust him, only trust him,
  Only trust him now;
He will save you, he will save you,
  He will save you now.

2 For Jesus shed his precious blood
    Rich blessings to bestow;
  Plunge now into the crimson flood
    That washes white as snow.

3 Yes, Jesus is the Truth, the Way,
    That leads you into rest;
  Believe in him without delay,
    And you are fully blest.

204 P. M.

COME to Jesus, come to Jesus,
  Come to Jesus just now;
Just now, come to Jesus,
  Come to Jesus, just now.

2 He will save you, etc.
3 He is able, etc.
4 He is willing, etc.
5 He is waiting, etc.
6 He will hear you, etc.
7 He will cleanse you, etc.
8 He'll renew you, etc.
9 He'll forgive you, etc.
10 If you trust him, etc.
11 He will save you, etc.

Trinity Supplement.

205 7s, 6 lines.

HALLELUJAH! who shall part
Christ's own Church from Christ's own
heart?
Sever from the Saviour's side
Souls for whom the Saviour died?
Dash one precious jewel down
From Immanuel's blood-bright crown?

2 Hallelujah! shall the sword
Part us from our glorious Lord?
Trouble dark or dire disgrace
E'er the Spirit's seal efface?
Famine, nakedness, or hate
Bride and bridegroom separate?

3 Hallelujah! life nor death,
Powers above, nor powers beneath,
Monarch's might nor tyrant's doom,
Things that are nor things to come,
Men nor angels e'er shall part
Christ's own Church from Christ's own heart!

206 8s, 7s, & 4.

HAST thou said, exalted Jesus,
Take thy cross and follow me?
Shall the word with terror seize us?
Shall we from the burden flee?
Lord, I'll take it,
And rejoicing follow thee.

2 While this liquid tomb surveying,
Emblem of my Saviour's grave,
Shall I shun its brink, betraying

Trinity Supplement.

Feelings worthy of a slave?
  No! I'll enter:
Jesus entered Jordan's wave.

3 Sweet the sign that thus reminds me,
  Saviour, of thy love to me;
Sweeter still the love that binds me
  In its deathless bond to thee:
    O what pleasure,
  Buried with my Lord to be!

4 Should it rend some fond connection,
  Should I suffer shame or loss,
Yet the fragrant, blest reflection,
  I have been where Jesus was,
    Will revive me
  When I faint beneath the cross.

5 Fellowship with him possessing,
  Let me die to all around;
So I rise t' enjoy the blessing
  Kept for those in Jesus found,
    When the archangel
  Wakes the sleeper under ground.

6 Then, baptized in love and glory,
  Lamb of God, thy praise I'll sing;
Loudly with the immortal story,
  All the harps of heaven shall ring,
    Saints and seraphs
  Sound it loud from every string.

207   C. M.

HOW sweet and awful is the place
  With Christ within the doors;
While everlasting love displays
  The choicest of her stores!

Trinity Supplement.

2 While all our hearts, and all our songs,
   Join to admire the feast,
Each of us cries, with thankful tongues,—
   "Lord, why was I a guest?"

3 "Why was I made to hear thy voice,
   And enter while there's room,
When thousands make a wretched choice,
   And rather starve than come?"

4 'Twas the same love that spread the feast,
   That sweetly drew us in;
Else we had still refused to taste,
   And perished in our sin.

208   8s & 7s.

IF you cannot on the ocean
   Sail among the swiftest fleet,
Rocking on the highest billows,
   Laughing at the storms you meet,
You can stand among the sailors
   Anchored yet within the bay;
You can lend a hand to help them
   As they launch their boats away.

2 If you are too weak to journey
   Up the mountain, steep and high,—
You can stand within the valley
   As the multitudes go by.
You can chant in happy measure
   As they slowly pass along;
Though they may forget the singer,
   They will not forget the song.

Trinity Supplement.

3 If you cannot in the conflict
   Prove yourself a warrior true,
If, where fire and smoke are thickest,
   There's no work for you to do,—
When the battle-field is silent,
   You can go with gentle tread,
You can bear away the wounded,
   You can cover up the dead.

4 Do not, then, stand idly waiting
   For some nobler work to do
For your heavenly Father's glory;
   Ever earnest, ever true,
Go and toil in any vineyard,
   Work in patience and in prayer;
If you *want* a field of labor,
   You can find it ANYWHERE.

209   6s & 8.

I GAVE my life for thee,
   My precious blood I shed,
That thou might'st ransomed be
   And quickened from the dead;
I gave, I gave My life for thee,
What hast thou given for me?

2 My Father's house of light,—
   My glory-circled throne
I left, for earthly night,
   For wand'rings sad and lone;
I left, I left it all for thee;
Hast thou left aught for Me?

3 I suffered much for thee,
   More than thy tongue can tell,
Of bitterest agony,

Trinity Supplement.

To rescue thee from hell;
I've borne, I've borne it all for thee,
What hast thou borne for Me?

4 And I have brought to thee,
   Down from My home above,
Salvation full and free,
   My pardon and My love;
I bring, I bring rich gifts to thee,
What hast thou brought to Me?

210   S. M.

I FAINT, my soul doth faint,
   My strength, a broken reed!
Would this so long be my complaint
   Were I a saint indeed?

2 The sins I fancied quell'd,
   Again in arms arise;
The promise that I thought I held
   Refuses its supplies.

3 My bosom burns with shame,
   And yet is icy cold;
Even to breathe the Saviour's name
   Seems now to be too bold.

4 So oft my soul had trod
   The same sad path astray,
How can I turn again to God?
   What venture now to say?

5 Thou, Saviour, only Thou
   Canst meet my utter need,
And should'st Thou save the rebel now,
   It will be grace indeed!

Trinity Supplement.

211 C. M.

IF God is mine, then present things,
  And things to come, are mine;
Yea, Christ, his word and Spirit too,
  And glory all divine.

2 If He is mine, then from His love
  He every trouble sends;
All things are working for my good,
  And bliss His rod attends.

3 If He is mine, I need not fear
  The rage of earth and hell;
He will support my feeble frame,
  Their utmost force repel.

4 If he is mine, let friends forsake;
  Let wealth and honors flee:
Sure He, who giveth me Himself,
  Is more than these to me.

5 If He is mine, I'll boldly pass
  Through death's tremendous vale;
He is a solid comfort when
  All other comforts fail.

6 O tell me, Lord, that Thou art mine;
  What can I wish beside?
My soul shall at the fountain live
  When all the streams are dried.

212 7s & 6s.

I LOVE to tell the story,
  Of unseen things above,
Of Jesus and his glory,
  Of Jesus and his love.

Trinity Supplement.

I love to tell the story
  Because I know 'tis true;
It satisfies my longings
  As nothing else can do.

  Cho.—I love to tell the story,
    'Twill be my theme in glory,
  To tell the old, old story,
    Of Jesus and his love.

2 I love to tell the story;
  More wonderful it seems
Than all the golden fancies
  Of all our golden dreams.
I love to tell the story,
  It did so much for me!
And that is just the reason
  I'll tell it now to thee.—*Cho.*

3 I love to tell the story;
  'Tis pleasant to repeat
What seems, each time I tell it,
  More wonderfully sweet.
I love to tell the story;
  For some have never heard
The message of salvation
  From God's own holy word.—*Cho.*

4 I love to tell the story;
  For those who know it best
Seem hungering and thirsting
  To hear it, like the rest.
And when, in scenes of glory,
  I sing the NEW, NEW SONG,
'T will be—the OLD, OLD STORY
  That I have loved so long.—*Cho.*

Trinity Supplement.

213   6s & 4s.

I NEED thee every hour,
  Most gracious Lord;
No tender voice like Thine
  Can peace afford.

REF.—I need Thee, O! I need Thee,
  Every hour I need Thee;
O bless me now, my Saviour!
  I come to Thee.

2 I need Thee every hour;
  Stay Thou near by:
Temptations lose their power
  When Thou art nigh.

3 I need Thee every hour,
  In joy or pain;
Come quickly and abide,
  Or life is vain.

4 I need Thee every hour;
  Teach me Thy will;
And Thy rich promises
  In me fulfill.

5 I need Thee every hour,
  Most Holy One;
O, make me Thine indeed,
  Thou blessed Son.

214   C. M.

I WORSHIP Thee, sweet Will of God!
  And all thy ways adore;
And every day I live, I long
  To love Thee more and more.

Trinity Supplement.

2 Man's weakness, waiting upon God,
   Its end can never miss,
For men on earth no work can do
   More angel-like than this.

3 He always wins who sides with God;
   To him no chance is lost;
God's will is sweetest to him when
   It triumphs at his cost.

4 Ill, that He blesses, is our good,
   And unblest good is ill;
And all is right that seems most wrong,
   If it be His dear will.

5 I love to kiss each print where Thou
   Hast set Thine unseen feet:
I cannot fear Thee, blessed Will,
   Thine empire is so sweet.

6 Though obstacles and trials seem
   Like prison walls to be;
I do the little I can do,
   And leave the rest to Thee.

7 I have no cares, O blessed Will,
   For all my cares are Thine;
I live in triumph, Lord, for Thou
   Hast made Thy triumphs mine.

215   P. M.

KNOCKING, knocking, who is there?
   Waiting, waiting, O, how fair!
'Tis a pilgrim, strange and kingly,
   Never such was seen before.
Ah! my soul, for such a wonder,
   Wilt thou not undo the door?

Trinity Supplement.

2 Knocking, knocking, still He's there,
Waiting, waiting, wondrous fair;
But the door is hard to open,
   For the weeds and ivy-vine,
With their dark and clinging tendrils,
   Ever round the hinges twine.

3 Knocking, knocking—what, still there?
Waiting, waiting, grand and fair;
Yes, the piercèd hand still knocketh,
   And beneath the crownèd hair
Beam the patient eyes, so tender
   Of thy Saviour waiting there.

216   8s, 7s, & 4.

LOOK, ye saints;—the sight is glorious;—
See the Man of sorrows now;
From the fight returned victorious,
   Every knee to Him shall bow;
     Crown Him, crown Him;
   Crowns become the Victor's brow.

2 Crown the Saviour, angels, crown Him;
   Rich the trophies Jesus brings;
In the seat of power enthrone Him
   While the heavenly concert rings:
     Crown Him, Crown Him;
   Crown the Saviour King of kings.

3 Sinners in derision crown Him,
   Mocking thus the Saviour's claim;
Saints and angels crowd around Him,
   Own His title, praise His name:
     Crown Him, crown Him;
   Spread abroad the Victor's fame!

Trinity Supplement.

4 Hark! these bursts of acclamation!
  Hark! these loud, triumphant chords!
Jesus takes the highest station;
  O, what joy the sight affords!
    Crown Him, crown Him,
  King of kings, and Lord of lords.

217   8s & 7s.

LORD, I hear of showers of blessing
  Thou art scattering full and free—
Showers the thirsty land refreshing:
  Let some droppings fall on me.

   CHORUS.—Even me, even me,
      Let thy blessing fall on me.

2 Pass me not, O gracious Father!
  Sinful tho' my heart may be;
Thou might'st leave me, but the rather
  Let thy mercy fall on me.

3 Pass me not, O tender Saviour!
  Let me love and cling to thee;
I am longing for thy favor;
  Whilst thou'rt calling, O call me.

4 Pass me not, O mighty Spirit!
  Thou can'st make the blind to see;
Witnesser of Jesus' merit,
  Speak the word of power to me.

5 Love of God, so pure and changeless;
  Blood of Christ, so rich and free;
Grace of God, so strong and boundless;—
  Magnify them all in me.

Trinity Supplement.

6 Pass me not! Thy lost one bringing,
    Bind my heart, O Lord, to thee;
While the streams of life are springing
    Blessing others, O bless me.

218   C. P. M.

LORD, thou hast won—at length I yield;
    My heart, by mighty grace compelled,
  Surrenders all to thee:
Against thy terrors long I strove,
But who can stand against thy love?—
  Love conquers even me.

2 Yes, since thou hast thy love reveal'd,
And shown my soul a pardon seal'd,
  I can resist no more;
Couldst thou for such a sinner bleed?
Canst thou for such a rebel plead?
  I wonder and adore!

3 If thou hadst bid thy thunders roll,
And lightnings flash to blast my soul,
  I still had stubborn been;
But mercy has my heart subdued,
A bleeding Saviour I have viewed,
  And now, I hate my sin.

4 Now, Lord, I would be thine alone—
Come, take possession of thine own,
  For thou hast set me free;
Released from Satan's hard command,
See, all my powers in waiting stand,
  To be employed by thee.

Trinity Supplement.

219 7s, 8 lines.

CHRIST, who came my soul to save,
Entered Jordan's yielding wave,
Rose from out the crystal flood,
Owned and sealed the Son of God.
By the Father's voice of love,
By the heaven descending Dove,
Saviour, Pattern, Guide for me,
I, like Him, baptized would be.

2 In the Garden, o'er his soul
Sorrow's whelming waves did roll;
Ah! on Calvary's cruel tree,
Jesus bowed in death for me.
I with him am crucified:
All my hope is—he hath died:
At his feet my place I take,
Bear the cross for his dear sake.

3 In the new-made tomb he lay,
Taking all its dread away;
Burst he through its rock-bound door,
Glorious now, and evermore.
I with Christ would buried be
In this rite required of me—
Rising from the mystic flood.
Living hence anew to God.

220 L. M.

O FOR a glance of heavenly day,
To take this stubborn heart away;
And thaw, with beams of love divine,
This heart, this frozen heart of mine.

Trinity Supplement.

2 The rocks can rend; the earth can quake;
The seas can roar; the mountains shake:
Of feeling, all things show some sign,
But this unfeeling heart of mine.

3 To hear the sorrows thou hast felt,
O Lord, an adamant would melt:
But I can read each moving line,
And nothing moves this heart of mine.

4 Thy judgments, too, which devils fear—
Amazing thought!—unmoved I hear;
Goodness and wrath in vain combine
To stir this stupid heart of mine.

5 But Power Divine can do the deed;
And, Lord, that power I greatly need:
Thy Spirit can from dross refine,
And melt and change this heart of mine.

221   C. P. M.

O LOVE divine, how sweet thou art!
  When shall I find my willing heart
    All taken up in thee?
I thirst, I faint, I die to prove
The greatness of redeeming love,
    The love of Christ to me.

2 Stronger his love than death or hell;
Its riches are unsearchable;
    The first-born sons of light
Desire in vain its depths to see;
They cannot reach the mystery,
    The length, the breadth, the height.

Trinity Supplement.

3 God only knows the love of God;
O that it now were shed abroad
  In this poor stony heart!
For this I sigh; for thee I pine;
This only portion, Lord, be mine,
  Be mine the better part!

222   C. M.

IN all my Lord's appointed ways
  My journey I'll pursue;
Hinder me not, ye much-loved saints!
  For I must go with you.

2 Through floods and flames, if Jesus leads,
  I'll follow where he goes;
Hinder me not! shall be my cry,
  Though earth and hell oppose.

3 Through duty, and through trials, too,
  I'll go at his command;
Hinder me not, for I am bound
  To my Immanuel's land.

4 And when my Saviour calls me home,
  Still this my cry shall be—
Hinder me not—come welcome death!
  I'll gladly go with thee.

223   P. M.

SAFE in the arms of Jesus,
  Safe on his gentle breast,
There by his love o'ershaded,
  Sweetly my soul shall rest.

Trinity Supplement.

Hark! 'tis the voice of angels,
   Borne in a song to me,
Over the fields of glory,
   Over the jasper sea.

CHORUS.—Safe in the arms of Jesus,
     Safe on his gentle breast,
   There by his love o'ershaded,
     Sweetly my soul shall rest.

2 Safe in the arms of Jesus,
   Safe from corroding care,
Safe from the world's temptations
   Sin cannot harm me there.
Free from the blight of sorrow,
   Free from my doubts and fears;
Only a few more trials,
   Only a few more tears!

3 Jesus, my heart's dear refuge,
   Jesus has died for me;
Firm on the Rock of Ages
   Ever my trust shall be.
Here let me wait with patience,
   Wait till the night is o'er;
Wait till I see the morning
   Break on the golden shore.

224   P. M.

SAVIOUR, more than life to me,
   I am clinging, clinging close to thee;
Let thy precious blood applied,
   Keep me ever, ever near thy side.

Trinity Supplement.

Ref.—Every day, every hour,
　　Let me feel thy cleansing power:
　　May thy tender love to me,
　　Bind me closer, closer, Lord, to thee.

2 Through this changing world below
Lead me gently, gently as I go.
Trusting thee, I cannot stray;
I can never, never lose my way.

3 Let me love thee more and more
Till this fleeting, fleeting life is o'er;
Till my soul is lost in love,
In a brighter, brighter world above.

225　　　　　8s & 7s.

SHALL we gather at the river
　　Where bright angel feet have trod,
With its crystal tide forever
　　Flowing by the throne of God?

Chorus.—Yes, we'll gather at the river,
　　The beautiful, the beautiful river—
　　Gather with the saints at the river,
　　That flows by the throne of God.

2 On the margin of the river,
　　Washing up its silver spray,
We will walk and worship ever
　　All the happy, golden day.

3 Ere we reach the shining river,
　　Lay we every burden down:
Grace our spirits will deliver,
　　And provide a robe and crown.

Trinity Supplement.

4 At the smiling of the river,
    Mirror of the Saviour's face,
Saints whom death will never sever,
    Lift their songs of saving grace.

5 Soon we'll reach the silver river,
    Soon our pilgrimage will cease;
Soon our happy hearts will quiver
    With the melody of peace.

226　　　　　　　　　　　P. M.

SOWING the seed by the daylight fair,
Sowing the seed by the noonday glare,
Sowing the seed by the fading light,
Sowing the seed in the solemn night;
   O, what shall the harvest be?
   O, what shall the harvest be?

CHORUS.—‖:Sown in the darkness or sown in
        the light,:‖
      ‖:Sown in our weakness or sown in
        our might,:‖
      Gathered in time or eternity,
        Sure, ah, sure will the harvest be.

2 Sowing the seed by the wayside high,
Sowing the seed on the rocks to die,
Sowing the seed where the thorns will spoil,
Sowing the seed in the fertile soil;
   O, what shall the harvest be?
   O, what shall the harvest be?

3 Sowing the seed of a lingering pain,
Sowing the seed of a maddened brain,

Trinity Supplement.

Sowing the seed of a tarnished name,
Sowing the seed of eternal shame;
  O, what shall the harvest be?
  O, what shall the harvest be?

4 Sowing the seed with an aching heart,
Sowing the seed while the tear-drops start,
Sowing in hope till the reapers come,
Gladly to gather the harvest home;
  O, what shall the harvest be?
  O, what shall the harvest be?

227   7s & 6s.

TELL me the Old, Old Story
  Of unseen things above,
Of Jesus and his glory,
  Of Jesus and his love.
Tell me the Story simply,
  As to a little child,
For I am weak and weary,
  And helpless and defiled.

CHORUS.—Tell me the Old, Old Story,
        Tell me the Old, Old Story,
        Tell me the Old, Old Story
        Of Jesus and his love.

2 Tell me the Story slowly,
  That I may take it in—
That wonderful redemption,
  God's remedy for sin.
Tell me the Story often,
  For I forget so soon!
The "early dew" of morning
  Has passed away at noon.—*Cho.*

Trinity Supplement.

3 Tell me the Story softly,
  With earnest tones and grave:
Remember! I'm the sinner
  Whom Jesus came to save.
Tell me that Story always
  If you would really be,
In any time of trouble,
  A comforter to me.—*Cho.*

4 Tell me the same Old Story
  When you have cause to fear
That this world's empty glory
  Is costing me too dear.
Yes, and when that world's glory
  Is dawning on my soul,
Tell me the Old, Old Story,
  "Christ Jesus makes thee whole."—*Cho.*

228   7s.

THOU art coming to a King,
  Large petitions with thee bring;
For His grace and power are such,
None can ever ask too much.

229   8s & 7s.

WE are living, we are dwelling,
  In a grand and awful time!
In an age on ages telling,
  To be living is sublime.
Hark! the waking up of nations,
  Gog and Magog to the fray.
Hark! what soundeth? is creation
  Groaning for its latter day?

Trinity Supplement.

2 Will ye play, then, will ye dally,
    With your music and your wine?
Up! it is Jehovah's rally!
    God's own arm had need of thine.
Hark! the onset! will ye fold your
    Faith-clad arms in lazy lock?
Up, O up, thou drowsy soldier;
    Worlds are charging to the shock.

3 Worlds are charging—heaven beholding;
    Thou hast but an hour to fight;
Now the blazoned cross unfolding,
    On—right onward, for the right.
On! let all the soul within you
    For the truth's sake go abroad!
Strike! let every nerve and sinew
    Tell on ages—tell for God!

230   8s & 7s.

WHAT a friend we have in Jesus,
    All our sins and griefs to bear;
What a privilege to carry
    Every thing to God in prayer.
O, what peace we often forfeit!
    O what needless pain we bear!
All because we do not carry
    Every thing to God in prayer.

2 Have we trials and temptations?
    Is there trouble anywhere?
We should never be discouraged,
    Take it to the Lord in prayer.
Can we find a Friend so faithful,
    Who will all our sorrows share?
Jesus knows our every weakness,
    Take it to the Lord in prayer.

Trinity Supplement.

3 Are we weak and heavy laden,
    Cumbered with a load of care?
Precious Saviour, still our refuge,
    Take it to the Lord in prayer.
Do thy friends despise, forsake thee?
    Take it to the Lord in prayer;
In his arms He'll take and shield thee,
    Thou wilt find a refuge there.

231   L. M., 6 lines.

WHAT means this eager, anxious throng,
    Which moves with busy haste along?
These wondrous gatherings day by day,
What means this strange commotion, pray?—
In accents hushed the throng reply,
"Jesus of Nazareth passeth by."

2 Who is this Jesus? why should he
The city move so mightily?
A passing stranger, has he skill
To move the multitude at will?
Again the stirring tones reply,
"Jesus of Nazareth passeth by."

3 Jesus! 'tis he who once below,
Man's pathway trod, 'mid pain and woe;
And burdened ones where'er he came,
Brought out their sick and deaf and lame;
The blind rejoiced to hear the cry,
"Jesus of Nazareth passeth by."

4 Again he comes from place to place,
His holy footprints we can trace;
He pauses at our threshold—nay,
He enters—condescends to stay;

Trinity Supplement.

Shall we not gladly raise the cry,
"Jesus of Nazareth passeth by?"

5 Ho! all ye heavy-laden, come;
Here's pardon, comfort, rest, and home.
Ye wanderers from a Father's face,
Return! accept his proffered grace:
Ye tempted ones there's refuge nigh,
"Jesus of Nazareth passeth by."

6 But if you still this call refuse,
And all his wondrous love abuse,
Soon will he sadly from you turn,
Your bitter prayer for pardon spurn.
"Too late! too late!" will be the cry,
"Jesus of Nazareth has passed by."

232　　　　　　　　7s, double.

WATCHMAN, tell us of the night,
　　What its signs of promise are:
Traveler, o'er yon mountain's height,
　See that glory-beaming star!
Watchman, does its beauteous ray
　Aught of hope or joy foretell?
Traveler, yes, it brings the day,
　Promised day of Israel.

2 Watchman, tell us of the night;
　Higher yet that star ascends:
Traveler, blessedness and light,
　Peace and truth, its course portends.
Watchman, will its beams alone
　Gild the spot that gave them birth?
Traveler, ages are its own;
　See, it bursts o'er all the earth.

Trinity Supplement.

3 Watchman, tell us of the night,
    For the morning seems to dawn:
Traveler, darkness takes its flight,
    Doubt and terror are withdrawn.
Watchman, let thy wanderings cease;
    Hie thee to thy quiet home:
Traveler, lo, the Prince of Peace,
    Lo, the Son of God is come!

233   8s, 7s, & 4.

ZION stands with hills surrounded—
Zion, kept by power divine;
All her foes shall be confounded,
    Though the world in arms combine;
        Happy Zion,
What a favored lot is thine!

2 Every human tie may perish;
    Friend to friend unfaithful prove;
Mothers cease their own to cherish;
    Heaven and earth at last remove;
        But no changes
Can attend Jehovah's love.

3 In the furnace God may prove thee,
    Thence to bring thee forth more bright,
But can never cease to love thee;
    Thou art precious in his sight;
        God is with thee—
God, thine everlasting light.

234

MY soul is not at rest. There comes a strange and secret whisper to my | spirit,‖ like a dream of | night,‖ that tells me I am on en- | chanted | ground.

Trinity Supplement.

CHORUS.—The voice of my departed Lord,
  "Go, teach all nations,"
  Comes on the night air and awakes
    mine ear.
  Through ages of eternal years,
  My spirit never shall repent,
  That toil and suffering once were
    mine below.

2 Why live I here? The vows of God are | on me,‖ and I may not stop to play with shadows or pluck earthly | flowers,‖ till I my work have done, and | rendered up ac- | count.—CHORUS.

3 And I will | go!‖ I may no longer doubt to give up friends and idle | hopes,‖ and every tie that binds my heart to | thee my | country!—CHORUS.

4 Henceforth, then, it matters not if storm or sunshine be my | earthly lot,‖ bitter or sweet my | cup,‖ I only pray, "God make me holy, and my spirit nerve for the stern | hour of | strife!"—CHORUS.

5 And when I come to stretch me for the | last,‖ in unattended agony, beneath the cocoa's | shade,‖ it will be sweet that I have toiled for | other worlds than | this.—CHORUS.

6 And if one, for whom Satan hath struggled as he hath for | me,‖ should ever reach that blessed | shore—‖ O, how this heart will glow with | gratitude and | love.

CHORUS.—Through ages of eternal years,
  My spirit never shall repent
  That toil and suffering once were
    mine below.

INDEX OF HYMNS.

	No.
A charge to keep I have............*Charles Wesley*	1
Alas! and did my Saviour bleed........*Isaac Watts*	2
Alas! what hourly dangers rise.......*Miss A. Steele*	3
All hail the power of Jesus'......*Edward Perronet*	4
Amazing grace! how sweet the sound..*John Newton*	5
Am I a soldier of the cross...............*Isaac Watts*	6
And will the Judge descend......*Philip Doddridge*	7
Approach, my soul, the mercy-seat....*John Newton*	8
Arise, my soul, arise................*Charles Wesley*	9
Arm of the Lord, awake, awake *William Shrubsole*	10
Around the throne of God in..*Mrs. A. H. Shepherd*	201
Awake, and sing the song......*William Hammond*	11
Awake, my soul, and with the sun.....*Thomas Ken*	12
Awake, my soul, in joyful lays......*Samuel Medley*	13
Awake, my soul, stretch every...*Philip Doddridge*	14
Before Jehovah's awful throne.........*Isaac Watts*	15
Behold a stranger at the door..........*Joseph Grigg*	16
Behold the Lamb of God.............*Alfred Taylor*	17
Be joyful in God, all ye lands....*James Montgomery*	18
Blest be the tie that binds.............*John Fawcett*	19
Blow ye the trumpet, blow...........*Charles Wesley*	20
Brightest and best of the sons of the.*Reginald Heber*	21
Broad is the road that leads to death....*Isaac Watts*	22
Calm me, my God, and keep me....*Horatius Bonar*	23
Child of sin and sorrow.......*Thos. Hastings*, (1832)	202
Children of the heavenly King........*John Cennick*	24
Christ is risen from the dead.........*Alfred Taylor*	25
Christ the Lord is risen to-day.......*Charles Wesley*	26
Christ who came my soul to save.......*S. D. Phelps*	219
Come, Christian brethren, ere we.......*H. K. White*	27
Come, come to Jesus...............*Rev. Geo. B. Peck*	28
Come, every pious heart...........*Samuel Stennett*	29
Come, every soul by sin.....*Rev. John H. Stockton*	203
Come, Holy Spirit, come................*Joseph Hart*	30
Come, Holy Spirit, heavenly Dove......*Isaac Watts*	31
Come, let us anew................*Charles Wesley*	32
Come, let us join our cheerful songs.....*Isaac Watts*	33
Come, let us sing the song......*James Montgomery*	34
Come, my Redeemer, come......*Rev. Andrew Reed*	35
Come, shout aloud the Father's.....*O. Heginbotham*	36
Come, sing to me of heaven.....*Mrs. M. S. B. Dana*	37
Come, thou Almighty King..........*Charles Wesley*	38

INDEX OF HYMNS.

	No.
Come, thou fount of every blessing......*R. Robinson*	39
Come to Jesus, come to Jesus..................*English*	204
Come, we who love the Lord............*Isaac Watts*	40
Come, ye disconsolate, where'er ye..*Thomas Moore*	41
Depth of mercy, can there be........*Charles Wesley*	42
Did Christ o'er sinners weep...*Benjamin Beddome*	43
Exalted Redeemer, almighty to save..*Alfred Taylor*	44
Forever with the Lord..........*James Montgomery*	45
Forth from the dark and stormy sky.*Reginald Heber*	46
From all that dwell below the skies......*Isaac Watts*	47
From every stormy wind that blows...*Hugh Stowell*	48
From Greenland's icy mountains...*Reginald Heber*	49
From the cross uplifted high........*Thomas Haweis*	50
Give to the winds thy fears...........*Paul Gerhardt*	51
Glory to God on high..................*James Allen*	52
God moves in a mysterious way....*William Cowper*	53
God with us! O glorious name........*Miss S. Slinn*	54
Glory be to the Father..........................*Bible*	200
Glory to thee, my God, this night.......*Thomas Ken*	55
Grace! 'tis a charming sound...*Philip Doddridge*	56
Gracious Spirit, love divine............*John Stocker*	57
Great Jehovah, we adore thee.................*Anon.*	58
Guide me, O thou great Jehovah.*William Williams*	59
Hail! my ever blessed Jesus.........*John Wingrove*	60
Hallelujah! who shall part......*William Dickinson*	205
Hark, my soul! it is the Lord......*William Cowper*	61
Hark, ten thousand harps and voices..*Thomas Kelly*	62
Hark! the song of jubilee......*James Montgomery*	63
Hark! the voice of Jesus calling.*Dan'l March, D.D.*	64
Hark! the voice of love and mercy.*Jonathan Evans*	65
Haste, my dull soul, arise......................*Anon.*	66
Hasten, sinner, to be wise............*Thomas Scott*	67
Haste, traveler, haste! the night....*Wm. B. Collyer*	68
Hast thou said, exalted Jesus...........*J. E. Giles*	206
He leadeth me! O blessed thought.*Jos. H. Gilmore*	69
Holy Father, hear me cry..........*Horatius Bonar*	70
Holy Ghost, with light divine..........*Andrew Reed*	71
Ho! my comrades, see the signal..........*P. P. Bliss*	72
How firm a foundation, ye saints of the....*Geo. Keith*	73
How helpless guilty nature lies..........*Miss A. Steele*	74
How pleasant thus to dwell below..............*Anon.*	75
How sad our state by nature is............*Isaac Watts*	76
How sweet and awful is the place........*Isaac Watts*	207
How sweet the name of Jesus sounds..*John Newton*	77
I'm a pilgrim, and I'm a stranger..*Mrs. M. S. B. Dana*	83
I'm but a stranger here..........*Thomas R. Taylor*	84
I faint, my soul doth faint........*Mrs. Ann Gilbert*	210

INDEX OF HYMNS.

	No.
If you cannot on the ocean........*Mrs. E. H. Gates*	208
I gave my life for thee........*Frances R. Havergal*	209
If God is mine, then present things......*B. Beddome*	211
I have a home, a glorious home......*Alfred Taylor*	78
I heard the voice of Jesus say.....*Horatius Bonar*	79
I hear my Saviour say................*Mrs. E. M. Hall*	80
I know that my Redeemer lives.....*Samuel Medley*	81
I lay my sins on Jesus...............*Horatius Bonar*	82
I love to tell the story..........*Kate Hankey*, (1867)	212
In all my Lord's appointed ways......*John Ryland*	222
I need thee every hour..............*Annie S. Hawks*	213
In the Christian's home in glory. *Rev. S. Y. Harmer*	85
I saw One hanging on a tree............*John Newton*	86
It is not death to die.........*Rev. Geo. W. Bethune*	87
I was a wand'ring sheep............*Horatius Bonar*	88
I worship thee, sweet will of God........*F. W. Faber*	214
I would not live alway............*W. A. Muhlenburg*	89
Jerusalem, my happy home ....*F. Baker*, (1616)	90
Jesus! and can it ever be...............*Joseph Grigg*	91
Jesus, I come to thee...............*Fanny J. Crosby*	92
Jesus, lover of my soul ....*Charles Wesley*	93
Jesus, my all, to heaven is gone.......*John Cennick*	94
Jesus only, when the morning........................*Nason*	95
Jesus shall reign where'er the sun ......*Isaac Watts*	96
Jesus, thy name I love........*Ryle's Sacred Songs*	97
Jesus, who knows full well ....*John Newton*	98
Joy to the world, the Lord is come......*Isaac Watts*	99
Just as I am, without one plea.....*Charlotte Elliott*	100
Just as thou art,—without one trace......*R. S. Cook*	101
King of glory, reign in me............*Alfred Taylor*	102
Knocking, knocking, who is there?.*Harriet B. Stowe*	215
Land ahead! Its fruits are waving..*Rev. E. Adams*	103
Look, ye saints; the sight is glorious....*Thos. Kelly*	216
Lo! on a narrow neck of land......*Charles Wesley*	104
Lord, dismiss us with thy blessing... *Walter Shirley*	105
Lord, I hear of showers of blessing.*Elizabeth Codner*	217
Lord, it belongs not to my care.....*Richard Baxter*	106
Lord, thou hast won—at length............*J. Newton*	218
Make haste, O man, to live........*Horatius Bonar*	107
'Mid scenes of confusion........*Rev. David Denham*	108
Mine eyes have seen the glory....*Julia Ward Howe*	109
More love to thee, O Christ........*Mrs. E. Prentiss*	110
Must Jesus bear the cross alone.*Rev. Tho. Shepherd*	111
My country! 'tis of thee......*Rev. Samuel F. Smith*	112
My days are gliding swiftly by.........*David Nelson*	113
My soul, be on thy guard.............*George Heath*	114
My soul is not at rest................*Nathan Brown*	234
My faith looks up to thee..............*Ray Palmer*	115
My Saviour stands waiting............*Alfred Taylor*	116

INDEX OF HYMNS.

		No.
Nearer, my God, to thee	Mrs. S. F. Adams	117
No merit of my own I bring	Alfred Taylor	118
Now begin the heavenly theme	Wm. Langford	119
Now I have found a friend	Henry J. McC. Hope	120
Now is the accepted time	John Dobell	121
O blessed message from on high	Alfred Taylor	122
O could I speak the matchless worth	Samuel Medley	123
O do not let the word depart	Hallowed Songs	124
O! for a closer walk with God	W. Cowper	125
O for a glance of heavenly day	Joseph Hart	220
O for a thousand tongues to sing	Charles Wesley	126
O happy day, that fix'd my choice	Philip Doddridge	127
On Jordan's stormy banks I stand	Samuel Stennett	128
O love divine, how sweet thou art	Charles Wesley	221
O speed thee, Christian! on thy way	Anon.	129
O that my load of sin were gone	Charles Wesley	130
O thou that hear'st when sinners cry	Isaac Watts	131
O thou who driest the mourner's tear	Thomas Moore	132
Our God, our help in ages past	Isaac Watts	133
Out on an ocean all boundless	Rev. W. F. Warren	134
O what hath Jesus done for me	Arr. from English	135
O where shall rest be found	J. Montgomery	136
O worship the king	Robert Grant	137
Palms of glory, raiment bright	J. Montgomery	138
Pass me not, O gentle Saviour	Fanny J. Crosby	139
Peace, troubled soul, whose plaintive	W. Shirley	140
Plunged in a gulf of dark despair	Isaac Watts	141
Praise God, from whom all blessings	Thomas Ken	142
Prayer is the soul's sincere desire	J. Montgomery	143
Repent! the voice celestial cries	Philip Doddridge	144
Return, O wanderer, return	W. B. Collyer	145
Rise, my soul, and stretch thy wings	R. Seagrave	146
Rock of ages, cleft for me	A. M. Toplady	147
Safe in the arms of Jesus	Fanny J. Crosby	223
Safely through another week	John Newton	148
Salvation! O the joyful sound	Isaac Watts	149
Saviour! I follow on	C. S. Robinson	150
Saviour, more than life to me	Fanny J. Crosby	224
Saviour, Prophet, Priest, and King	Alfred Taylor	151
Saviour! thy dying love	S. D. Phelps	153
Saviour, visit thy plantation	John Newton	152
Say, sinner, hath a voice within	Mrs. A. B. Hyde	154
Shall we gather at the river	Robert Lowry, (1864)	225
Show pity, Lord, O Lord, forgive	Isaac Watts	155
Sinner, rouse thee from thy sleep	Episcopal Coll.	156
Sinners, turn; why will ye die	Charles Wesley	157
Soldiers of Christ, arise	Charles Wesley	158
So let our lips and lives express	Isaac Watts	159

INDEX OF HYMNS.

	No.
Sowing the seed by the daylight. *Emily S. Oakey*, (1850)	226
Stand up, my soul, shake off thy fears... *Isaac Watts*	160
Stand up for Jesus, Christian.. *R. Torrey, Jr.*, (1869.)	161
Stand up!—stand up for Jesus....... *George Duffield*	162
Stay, thou insulted Spirit, stay....... *Charles Wesley*	163
Sun of my soul, thou Saviour dear........ *John Keble*	164
Sweet hour of prayer........... *Rev. W. W. Walford*	165
Tell me the Old, Old Story...... *Kate Hankey*, (1867)	227
Ten thousand times ten thousand.... *Rev. H. Alford*	166
The Lord descended from.... *Thos. Sternhold*, (1549)	167
The Lord Jehovah reigns................ *Isaac Watts*	168
The Lord shall come! the earth.... *Reginald Heber*	169
The morning light is breaking............. *S. F. Smith*	170
There is a fountain filled with blood..... *W. Cowper*	171
There is a land of pure delight........... *Isaac Watts*	172
There is a name I love to hear.. *Frederick Whitfield*	173
The Spirit in our hearts........... *H. U. Onderdonk*	174
Thine earthly Sabbaths, Lord.... *Philip Doddridge*	175
This is not my place of resting...... *Horatius Bonar*	176
Thou art coming to a king............. *John Newton*	228
To-day the Saviour calls.................. *S. F. Smith*	177
Vain, delusive world, adieu.......... *Charles Wesley*	178
Wait, my soul, upon the Lord... *W. Freeman Lloyd*	179
Walk in the light! so shalt thou... *Bernard Barton*	180
Watchman, tell us of the night.......... *J. Bowring*	232
We are living, we are dwelling............. *A. C. Coxe*	229
Weary sinner! keep thine eyes................. *Anon.*	181
Welcome, sweet day of rest............. *Isaac Watts*	182
Welcome, welcome, dear Redeemer.. *Rev. W. Mason*	183
We praise thee, O God, for the Son of.. *W. P. Mackay*	184
We've 'listed in a holy war........ *Fanny J. Crosby*	185
What a Friend we have in Jesus............ *H. Bonar*	230
What means this eager, anxious.. *Emma Campbell*	231
When all thy mercies, O my God... *Joseph Addison*	186
When gathering clouds around I view.. *Robert Grant*	187
When I can read my title clear.......... *Isaac Watts*	188
When marshalled on the nightly plain,.. *H. K. White*	189
With tearful eyes I look around... *Charlotte Elliott*	190
When thou, my righteous Judge...... *Selina Shirley*	191
While life prolongs its precious.... *Timothy Dwight*	192
Who are these in bright array........ *J. Montgomery*	193
Why will ye waste on trifling...... *Philip Doddridge*	194
With one consent let all the earth...... *Nahum Tate*	195
Work, Christian laborer, work....... *Alfred Taylor*	196
Work, for the night is coming..... *Sidney Dyer, alt.*	197
Ye servants of God.................. *Charles Wesley*	198
Your harps, ye trembling saints..... *A. M. Toplady*	199
Zion stands with hills surrounded....... *Thos. Kelly*	233

www.ingramcontent.com/pod-product-compliance
Lightning Source LLC
Chambersburg PA
CBHW032146160426
43197CB00008B/787